NEGOTIATING
from the
INSIDE OUT

NEGOTIATING
from the
INSIDE OUT

A Playbook for
Business Success

CLINT BABCOCK
Foreword by DAVID MATTSON

Paperback: 978-1-7351472-0-8

E-book: 978-1-7351472-1-5

*This book is dedicated to
my wonderful wife Donna,
without whose support
and encouragement it
would not exist.*

Contents

PART 3: Supercharge Your Playbook

Acknowledgments

Every book that reaches its intended audience is to some degree a collaboration, and this one more than most.

I owe deep thanks to my wife Donna, whose unfailing support and encouragement made this project possible; to my brilliant twin daughters, Alyssa and Jolie, who inspire me at every turn; to my parents, Steve and May, for teaching me to work hard, do the right thing, and to have confidence in myself; to my two brothers, Steve and Scott, for providing the physical and mental conditioning that only two loving brothers could give; to my business partner, Jim Marshall, for showing me that attitude truly is everything and for his invaluable guidance, direction, and certainty that everything would be OK, even when I had my doubts; to my Sandler coach, Bill Art, for being the mentor that I needed; to the Oracle of Baltimore, Dave Mattson, whose forward-thinking leadership style I've tried to emulate since the first Sandler conference I attended back in June 2005; to Yusuf Toropov, my editor; to Rob Fishman, Coach Brad McDonald, Tim and Katie Roberts, Jim and Joan Stephens, Mike Crandall, Suzie Andrews, Andrew Gieselmann, Jim Wilcox, Kevin Hallenbeck, Andrew Wall, and Jeff Pankoff, all of whom, as members of the Diamonds Group, challenge me every day to become better at what I do; and to Rachel Miller, Margaret Stevens Jacks, Laura Matthews, Jerry Dorris, Lori Ames, and Shannon Haaf Howell, all of whom provided essential support and worked hard over a long period of time in support of this project.

Foreword

Years ago, I was teaching a two-day negotiation program for a large financial insti-
tution. This client was enrolling employees
from various divisions across the company, with locations on different coasts, to take part in the Sandler
negotiating program. At the last minute, I got a call
from a contact at the company, who informed me
that they wanted to negotiate us down on the price.
They were paying us per person and suddenly realized
they were going to be paying for a lot of people—
about 400 in all were scheduled to be in the room.
My contact wanted us to agree to a lower per person
rate. Ironically, I was being hired to teach them not to
negotiate on pricing.

This, I realized, was a classic moment of truth—a
moment when I had to decide for myself if I was going
to walk my talk. I explained to my contact that I would
be a hypocrite and a fraud if I agreed to negotiate on

the price. Then, I told him that I had a suggestion. We could cancel (but they would need to cancel hundreds of plane tickets and hotel nights) or—better yet—I could throw in an added service. I knew that, eventually, they were going to ask us to provide management training, so I offered to stay an extra day to cover management, which they could then reinforce with the people who took the program.

He agreed. We ended up keeping the per-person price as it was. They were happy, I was happy—and I didn't have to negotiate pricing. Not only that, I had a great addition to the program that I wouldn't have otherwise had. I used that very story to land the point with them—and later with countless other clients—never to negotiate price, but to instead negotiate service.

I believe that, sooner or later, salespeople all face major moments of truth when it comes to negotiating. Clint Babcock's book covers them all. It gives the tools to effectively respond, in real time, to any of the major gambits. Just as important, Babcock's book shows how to address the biggest challenges to constructive negotiation that any of us face: our own internal attitudes and beliefs. *Negotiating from the Inside Out* is a powerful summary of the core Sandler principles for successful negotiating outcomes. Read it, practice it, reinforce it, and use it to turn your own moment of truth into a moment of mutual success.

David Mattson
President/CEO, Sandler Training

Introduction

Many of the business leaders and sales professionals my company works with tell us they are frustrated by:

◆ A total lack of process when it comes to negotiation. When we ask them what their internal negotiation system is, they shake their heads and admit that they don't have such a system for their people to follow.

◆ Team members who routinely negotiate against themselves, offering price cuts and other major concessions without even being asked to do so by the other side.

◆ Margins that get undermined or destroyed altogether by negotiators who ask for and receive major concessions from team members who don't realize they're being played.

If one or more of these issues arises in your world, you may want to keep reading. I wrote this book to help teams and organizations recognize and overcome all of these challenges.

Let's get started.

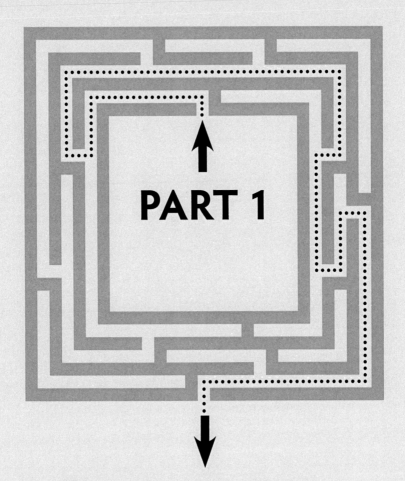

PART 1

The Inner Game
of Negotiating

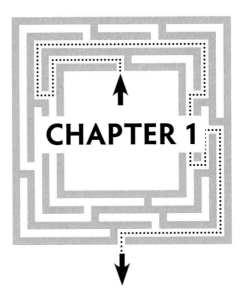

CHAPTER 1

Start with the Mirror

I t's all about you (at first).

Years ago, I was the regional manager for a technology training company, overseeing five locations. We were a small division of a $5 billion technology and printing firm. My world shifted a bit when my division was sold to a private equity firm. One of the first initiatives of the new company's leadership was to "consolidate accounting systems." Translation: We had to move our local accounting function to our new corporate office. We had to use their software and stop using the software we were used to. This was a major transition, and we had our issues. One of the biggest challenges had to do with invoicing our customers. We experienced over four months of invoicing chaos—sometimes invoices went out incorrectly, sometimes they went out too late, and sometimes they didn't go out at all.

By the time we started to get a handle on the problem, our account receivables had ballooned. I found myself spending a lot of time calling on our customers to apologize and work through all the mistakes. One of our largest customers, a well-known national bank, had asked us to come in so we could figure out some way out of the maze. By our count, which we had double- and triple-checked, they owed us a little over a hundred thousand dollars. Yet the invoicing had been so problematic and the mistakes so complex that their finance and training people still had a lot of questions. Suffice to say that this was an important meeting. My marketplace manager spent days preparing the data, and we both invested a lot of time getting ready.

As we sat in their conference room at their headquarters, handouts at the ready, awaiting the arrival of their vice president of training and development, we chatted with three of the bank's other team members. We talked about the weather. We talked about the local sports team. You get the picture: Happy talk. Casual chitchat. All of a sudden, in walks the VP. The atmosphere instantly changes. The three people we've been chatting with stop smiling and start frowning.

The VP doesn't say hello, he doesn't sit down, and he doesn't make eye contact. He stands at the head of the table and says, "Look, you guys have already cost us so much time trying to figure out your invoices, which classes we have taken, and which ones we haven't that I don't believe we should pay you anything. However, here's what we've been able to figure out on our side. We owe you about $70,000. We'll pay you $70,000 within the next week and call it even and then move forward. Now, I've got to go to another meeting. It's a busy day here and I don't have any more time for this. Just let us know what you decide."

There was a split-second pause, and during that pause he made eye contact with me for the very first time. As he did, I'm sure he sensed the fear that his words had brought about in me. That, of course, was his desired outcome.

Having produced that outcome, he turned and walked out of the room. Negotiation over. Suffice it to say, I was unprepared to deal with someone like him.

As I reflect upon that situation, I can't help remembering the depth of the panic and stress I experienced in that moment. I can't help thinking about how little I had done to prepare myself—not just tactically, but mentally and emotionally—for that meeting. That VP didn't beat me at the negotiating table—I beat me.

Today, I realize I would have had a much better outcome had I had the strong belief and mindset that our information was correct. It was; we had all our ducks in a row. But deep down, I felt my leverage was not very strong because I knew that we were the ones who had caused the invoicing issues. My belief structure and my mental and emotional starting point were all wrong. As a result, I walked in the door hoping to please. I began the meeting at a disadvantage.

Not only that: I didn't recognize the tactic being used on me for what it was—a tactic. If I had been able to recognize the negotiations gambit the VP had just used to take me off guard—a quick and decisive demand, followed by an apparent collapse of discussions—I could have responded to it much more effectively than I did. Knowing what you are likely to be up against is a critical part of the mental "game" of negotiation. The knowledge you have makes it more likely that you will respond maturely and resourcefully in a potentially stressful situation.

Finally, even though I was prepared with all the data as I walked into that room, I look back now and realize how unprepared I was tactically. I had been totally caught off guard, with no response at the ready, because I hadn't realized that the "game" could begin at any moment. It didn't occur to me to have a response ready just in case someone threw me a curveball. I was literally speechless. The moment of truth came during the instant that he looked at me for a response, and I was completely unprepared. I collapsed. That collapse was entirely preventable. If I had done a better job of preparing tactically, I would not have caved at the moment of truth and he could not have taken advantage of me in the way that he did.

What I want you to notice is that it was my own choices and my own internal responses that caused me to get crushed in that negotiation—such as it was. And, there were lots of people counting on me. I had let down not just myself but my whole team.

I tell you this story for a simple reason: The best place to begin any discussion about negotiation is by consulting the nearest mirror.

You have to start with yourself. At the beginning, at least, it is really all about you: what you choose to do and not do before entering a negotiation discussion, how you think about yourself and the world around you, and whether you respond consciously or react heedlessly and emotionally at the moment of truth. In this first chapter, we'll look closely at the only thing you truly have total control over in any negotiating situation: the mind and emotions of the person you see staring back at you when you look in the mirror.

How You Defeat Yourself

Negotiation is a skill. The first thing you have to do to improve that skill is to understand your own current skill level, how you react to pressure situations, and how you negotiate for yourself and for your companies. Always begin with where you are right now. Where I was at the moment that that VP beat me was a place called, "I am not enough."

This is the most common way to defeat yourself in negotiations. If you don't approach the negotiating discussion as a peer, you will lose.

In my case, I was beginning the exchange from a position of subservience, of deficiency. This left me unable to manage my own emotions, and as a result, I lost the negotiating encounter. Maybe the same thing has happened to you. To illustrate the nature of that deficiency, I'd like to do a little imaginative exercise with you.

What's your emotional bounce back rate when something in business goes wrong? Do you take it personally when you are rejected in business, lose a deal, or receive constructive criticism from a manager or client? As you start to look inward, it's important to understand Identity/Role Theory, which can help you not only become a better negotiator, but show you how to deal with outcomes that may not be in your favor.

First, the easy part: roles. Everyone has a lot of roles to play in life: spouse, employee, sibling, athlete, student, child. At any moment during the day, people are moving in and out of these roles. If you've just left work and your best friend calls you, you immediately and smoothly transition from "employee" into "friend" role. Understanding this, there are times when you are awesome at these roles, and there are times you might struggle or fail.

The same goes for you as a negotiator. Therefore, it's important to spend time working on these roles. If you want to become a better athlete, then you practice, practice, practice. If you want to become a better life partner, then you'll put in the time and change your behaviors in order to be better. However, if you fail at these roles, does this affect your core values and how you think and believe about yourself? Although no one likes to fail, understand that everyone does at one time or another. As long as you don't let that affect your belief in yourself, you'll be ensuring that you consistently perform at a high level in your roles because of a strong identity.

However, if you aren't aware of how you are seeing yourself internally, your identity, then you'll struggle to consistently perform well in your roles. Your identity is your core values, your self-esteem and self-image, and your inner mindset. It's that voice that tells you you're a solid person of character and values who wants the best for other people and for yourself. Because of this, your ability to perform well in your roles is directly correlated to how you see yourself in your identity. People who have a strong identity belief will fail at times in their roles; however, because of their self-image, they won't let a failure affect their internal belief in themselves. They'll begin to work on how to improve in their role to avoid another role failure.

Do you know someone who doesn't think very highly of themselves? Someone who routinely talks down about not only themselves, but tends to bring others down with them as well? What about the person who makes excuses and doesn't accept responsibility for their own failure, and, when they win, they think victory is just one of those things that happens? Oh, and how about the person you may know who feels like the world is stacked against them because of something that may have happened to them in their past? These people will usually have a low sense of identity and self-worth and therefore will consistently perform poorly in their roles. At the very least, they will have inconsistent patterns of ups and downs. They don't believe they deserve the ups in their life, so they'll self-sabotage their wins to get themselves back in line with their non-winner identity.

On the other hand, seeing yourself internally as a winner will enhance your role as a negotiator. If you enter into a negotiation with the right mindset about yourself, you'll consistently perform as a winner at the negotiation table. You'll be able to use the tactics and strategies outlined in this book because you will have the drive to learn more, which strengthens the mind and prepares you to perform. For a real world example of how Identify/Role Theory works, consider the following example (maybe you have experienced something like this). In the recession of 2007–2009, companies were laying off people every day. The unemployment rate in the United States jumped from just under 5% to over 10%. Or consider the pandemic of 2020, which, among many other dire effects, caused unemployment to reach even higher levels through both layoffs and furloughs. Did you, or someone you knew, lose their job for no other reason than companies slashing headcount? This could be you, or it could be a friend or family member—even a parent. Think of that person now—or put yourself in the position of someone facing that situation.

That individual lost their job not because of their performance, but because the company had to downsize. After having an identity associated with what they did for a living that was not there anymore, many felt depressed and unsure about who they were. They identified themselves so much with what they did for a living (their role) that they confused the two. When the role no longer existed, the person struggled with their self-belief and value. But what you do for a living is not your identity. It's a role, and roles change. Odds are, you have had a few different roles in your career, but your identity was not left behind in your last job.

During that earlier recession, I was consistently asked to deliver job prospecting and interviewing talks to numerous groups of unemployed people, sometimes numbering in the hundreds. Some of these people had been out of work for 6–12 months and had barely been able to secure a single interview. I would share with them certain strategies about how to find the hidden jobs that are not advertised, how to network better and build a network, how to use LinkedIn, and how to handle interviews. I gave them a lot of tactics. Then, I would always end my talk explaining Identity/Role Theory. This concept consistently resonated more powerfully with everyone than anything else I discussed. It was a silent internal challenge they couldn't describe, but they knew was there. I was just able to put their feelings into terms that they could understand and easily grasp.

Separating your identity from your role is, from one perspective, the work of a lifetime. It's not something you grasp and forget about. It's something you keep working on over time. It's something you have to practice continually.

Put on your buyer's hat for a moment. Do you find

yourself trying to negotiate on a regular basis? I'm not just talking about typical situations like buying a car or a house. I'm talking about negotiating at the golf course for a foursome, your dry-cleaner for a deadline, your cable bill for a discount, or even your vacation with the family for an extra treat. I believe the better negotiator you are as a buyer, the stronger a negotiator you will be as a seller.

What you will learn as you move forward in this book is that there are certain gambits buyers use to create leverage. The better you are at recognizing and using these buyer strategies and the more practice you give yourself at separating your role from your identity, the better you will be at responding to buyer strategies when someone tries to use them against you.

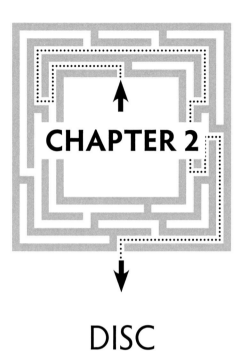

CHAPTER 2

DISC

The best negotiators always start negotiation by negotiating with themselves. This means understanding whether the self-talk in your mind develops your confidence and your sense of self-worth or undermines you. It also means getting to know your own communication and behavioral style, which has a lot to do with how you think and react under pressure. One of the communication tools that will help you better understand yourself and how others communicate with you is called DISC.

If you haven't heard of DISC, it's time to become familiar with it. If you have heard it, it's time for a deeper dive. This will be painless, I promise.

Fill in the blanks below, associating each sentence with people you know.

Profile #1

"I'm a self-starter and a born risk-taker. I love solving problems. People say I have a healthy ego. I am direct in my dealings with you. I live to make decisions. My secret fear is that someone will take advantage of me."

A colleague who fits this description is

_____.

A prospect or client who fits this description is

_____.

Profile #2

"I'm extremely enthusiastic, talkative, and persuasive. I draw energy from groups and thrive in social situations. I motivate others to achieve at a high level. I am usually optimistic. People sometimes say I'm too emotional. At my best, I'm downright inspirational. My secret fear is rejection."

A colleague who fits this description is

_____.

A prospect or client who fits this description is

_____.

Profile #3

"I'm a great listener, loyal to the end, and eager to understand you. Some people call me the ultimate team player. Relationships mean a lot to me, and I don't like to let an ally down. I'm a peacekeeper. I'm reliable and dependable. My biggest fear is a loss of security."

A colleague who fits this description is

_____.

A prospect or client who fits this description is

_____.

Profile #4

"I have high standards. I work systematically. I'm precise. I find out the facts. I'm cautious, careful, and conscientious. I'm rigorously analytical. It's extremely important to me to be accurate and well-organized. My secret fear is being forced to choose between quality and relationships because I will lean toward quality."

A colleague who fits this description is

_____.

A prospect or client who fits this description is

_____.

And now for the big question:

The profile that most closely describes me is:
#1, #2, #3, or #4.

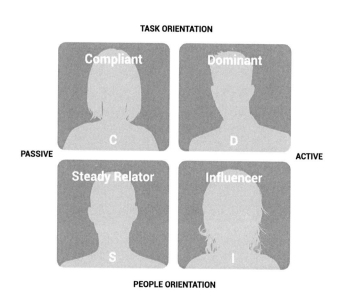

- People you aligned with Profile #1 are likely Dominants.
- People you aligned with Profile #2 are likely Influencers.
- People you aligned with Profile #3 are likely Steady Relators.
- People you aligned with Profile #4 are likely Compliants.

Now for the big question: Which style did you identify as your own?

If you're like most of the people we work with, one profile jumped out at you as instinctive, as natural, as "normal." In reality, there is no normal, but there are means of communicating, behaving, and interacting that feel intuitive to us. Which of the four styles felt most intuitive to you?

As you read through these descriptions of the four DISC behavioral styles, confirm whether your initial guess about your own style matches up with the summaries.

A Dominant is:

- Aggressive.
- Blunt.
- Bottom-line oriented.
- Results oriented.
- Impatient.
- Easily irritated.
- Demanding.
- Competitive.
- Fond of change.
- Goal oriented.

An Influencer is:

- Talkative.

- Animated.
- Easily excited.
- Open and friendly.
- Unorganized.
- Known for a short attention span.
- Constantly jumping from subject to subject.
- A collaborative decision maker.
- Positive.

A Steady Relator is:

- Easygoing.
- Calm.
- A careful listener.
- Thoughtful.
- Someone who needs time to process information.
- Someone who asks questions.
- Opinionated, but does not express opinions openly.
- Resistant to change.
- Resistant to risk.
- Attracted to mutually fair solutions.

A Compliant is:

- Facts-oriented.
- An analyzer.
- Fond of rules.
- Responsive to instruction.

- Quiet.
- Someone who asks many questions.
- Reserved and timid.
- A researcher.
- An examiner of specifics.
- Resistant to personal criticism.

So—which one of the four styles feels most like you? Have you got a clear sense of that now?

Each of the four behavioral styles is like a language unto itself. The more languages you speak and the more fluently you speak them, the more effective your interactions with others will be and the more success you will have as a negotiator. Think of it this way: Most people only speak one DISC language—their own. They tell themselves that they simply "don't connect" or "can't connect" with certain types of people. Most people buy into that kind of negative self-talk, and, as a result, they interact imperfectly and inefficiently with roughly 75% of the population. How much more could they accomplish if they spoke all four of the DISC languages?

For my part, I am a Steady Relator. Most of us are non-confrontational by nature. Not only that, we avoid taking risks, we love being part of a team, and we are not happy about change. Now, one of the prospects I was dealing with a few years back was a woman I'll call Georgianna, who was a nice high Dominant—strong in that quadrant—which meant her natural inclinations were in the exact opposite direction of mine. She was very comfortable confronting people, happy to take risks in pursuit of a goal, enjoyed making decisions on her own, and loved shaking things up.

Georgianna and I got to a point in the sales process where I said to her, "You're probably going to want to take this outline we've put together back to your team so you can talk with them and get their feedback, and you can decide what you feel most comfortable doing. Meanwhile, I'll talk to my team about this. And we'll meet next week." Classic Steady Relator: I am a team player, and I assumed she was also. Why wouldn't she be?

Because she's a high Dominant!

Georgianna said, "Clint, I've got a better idea. I've already talked to my team. They're on board with this. Let me tell you what's going to happen if we wait a week. You're going to come back with a number, I'm not going to like it, I'm going to tell you to come off that number, you're going to change the program a little bit so you can justify coming off of that number, and then we're going to do business together. So why don't we just save each other some time and energy and do all of that right now, you and me?"

That's what we did! If I had followed my inclinations rather than hers, the inclination of both of us going back to our respective teams and talking things over, I would have slowed down my sales cycle and eventually gotten exactly the same outcome. Because I was open to the tendencies and priorities of the Dominant, because I wasn't intimidated by them, I was willing to recognize a time when it made sense to step away from my usual process (note that Steady Relators love structure) and to start speaking Georgianna's language.

Now that you have identified your communication style, you are in a better position to understand the best ways to connect with others and to prioritize what is likely to be most important to them.

Remember, as a negotiator you need to understand the other person's point of view and how they operate. Below is a summary of things to do if you are a D, I, S, or C and are dealing with someone of another style. (If you're the same style as the person you're working with, go ahead and just be yourself.)

Dominant

- Be more patient.
- Talk less, listen more.
- Allow time for "small talk."
- Slow down your presentation.
- Focus more on feelings and emotions.
- Be careful not to dominate the interaction.

- Be careful not to come across as blunt or impolite.

Influencer

- Be more direct.
- Keep to the subject.
- Talk less, listen more.
- Remember to follow up.
- Do not get too emotional.
- Slow down your presentation.
- Focus more on details and facts.
- Be careful not to move too close to others.

Steady Relator

- Talk more.
- Focus a little less on details.
- Speed up your presentation.
- Keep emotions under control.
- Be more expressive and animated.
- Be careful not to come across as too opinionated.
- Be more results-oriented in your communication.

Compliant

- Talk more.
- Be more expressive.
- Spend more time chatting.
- Focus on being more inspiring.

- Speak more about people and emotions.
- Talk less about detail, facts, and figures.
- Be careful not to appear cold, impolite, and distant.

Think of how powerful it is to be able to enter any negotiating situation with the confidence that since you understand communication styles, you are in a much better position to control the direction of the conversation.*

You can always adjust your communication style to suit the occasion—and the person you are working with.

---

* This is true in both one-on-one and group settings. Note that in those situations where you happen to find yourself in communication with multiple influencers at the same time, your best strategy is going to be to identify and accommodate the DISC style of the senior decision maker.

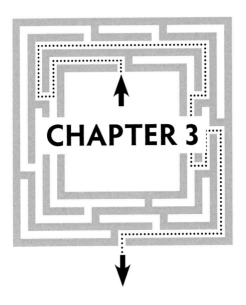

CHAPTER 3

TA and the Drama Triangle

I t will come as no surprise that the best negotiators are those who are most deeply acquainted with the principles of human psychology. Perhaps the most important school of psychology for anyone aspiring to become a truly effective negotiator is transactional analysis (TA).*

TA was developed by the psychologist Dr. Eric Berne in the late 1950s. Berne noticed that his patients, and

---

* The summary of TA in this chapter is adapted from Sandler Training's *Gold Medal Selling*.

indeed all people, could and would change over the course of a single conversation. The changes were both verbal and non-verbal, including facial expressions, body language, body temperature, and other cues.

Berne's breakthrough came when he was counselling a 35-year-old lawyer. The two were discussing something the lawyer had done that he had regretted. Berne asked him, "Why then did you do it?" The lawyer explained that, although part of him hadn't wanted to do what he'd done, "...the child inside me made me do it."

Out of this conversation, Berne developed the TA psychological model. Berne theorized that three influences live within each person: the ego states of the Parent, the Adult, and the Child. Let's look at each of these now.

The Parent Ego State

The Parent ego state acts like an audio recorder, storing lessons and messages people received from their parents and other authority figures from birth until they were about six. This recording cannot be erased.

Sometimes, those messages were communicated in a stern, authoritarian, critical manner (Critical Parent). Examples of recordings in the Critical Parent include: "Never talk to strangers," and "How many times have I told you not to do that?" At other times those messages were communicated in a more nurturing manner

(Nurturing Parent) as helpful suggestions and supportive words. Examples of recordings in the Nurturing Parent include: "You always try your best, and that is always good enough," and "Don't worry that you made a mistake today. You can always learn a lesson when you make a mistake."

These Parent recordings play back at different times in a person's life after the age of five, and they become beliefs that the person then creates within themselves. For adults, these lessons/messages are usually stored as "what-to-do's"—right/wrong, do/don't, should/shouldn't—and largely control judgments and behavior.

These judgments and behaviors are triggered when adults are faced with something that reminds them of interactions involving their parents or other authority figures or of ways they dealt with or assigned meaning to the actions of parents or authority figures in their lives.

The Adult Ego State

The Adult ego state starts recording at about nine months, continues to record throughout people's entire lives, and filters all the information they receive. Responding to what is happening in the present, people think, feel, and behave as an adult, meaning they use the expanding resource of their own accumulated life experience to guide their decision making.

The Adult ego state is always rational and analytical

and updates information as it is received. It includes two additional elements: the Updated Parent and the Updated Child (for a discussion of the Child ego state, see below). As the name suggests, the Updated Parent allows people to upgrade the warnings they heard in childhood from the Critical Parent. For example, warnings like, "Don't talk to strangers." Through the Updated Parent, people can update those belief systems and change the way they think about things. For instance, an updated "Don't talk to strangers" belief might be: "Most people I meet are friendly and interesting, they want to engage with me, and they are eager to talk about themselves. It's exciting to speak to new people, and when I do I generally uncover new opportunities." In a similar way, the Updated Child allows people to update the way they feel about things.

The Child Ego State

The Child ego state is also a recorder that is activated at birth and turns off at about age six. Here are all the feelings that have ever festered inside of a person in response to the ancient Parent recordings: the rights and wrongs, the shoulds and shouldn'ts, and the do's and don'ts that Mom, Dad, and other caregivers were speaking, shouting, or commanding.

This inner voice of the Child cannot be erased, but,

like the Parent recordings, people can choose to update it with more empowering and positive messages that then translate into new belief systems. The Child ego state has four components:

- Adaptive Child: Longing to please the Parent recordings and always seeking approval.
- Rebellious Child: Angry and fearful, often selfish, and always ready and waiting for a fight.
- Natural Child: Playful and creative, uninhibited and spontaneous, and likes fun and laughter.
- Little Professor (combination of Rebellious and Natural Child): Very manipulative to meet its own needs and not very authentic.

In negotiating interactions—indeed, in all interactions—the optimal effective communication, according to TA, is for a person to come from the Nurturing Parent and Adult ego states as frequently as possible. Ideally, 70% of effective communication comes from the Nurturing Parent and 30% is from the Adult ego state. In regard to the other ego states, we have a negotiating rule[*] to pass along: Leave the Child in the car and send the Critical Parent on a one-way ticket to outer space.

A word is probably in order here about the whole idea

---

[*] All of the negotiating rules in this book arise from the famous Sandler Rules for selling, developed by David Sandler, the founder of Sandler training.

of negotiating rules. I will be sharing many of these with you in this book. Many people ask me whether it ever makes sense to break one of the negotiating rules found in these pages. My answer is: If you know what a given rule is and why it is there, you are much more likely to understand when and why it might make sense to break the rule. Breaking a negotiating rule should be a conscious decision—one you don't make lightly. Think of this decision as being a little like the decision to exceed the speed limit while driving. Do even good drivers do that sometimes? The answer, of course, is yes. Do they only break the rule when they feel personally confident that it is safe to do so? Again, the answer is yes.

NEGOTIATING RULE

Leave the Child in the car—and send the Critical Parent on a one-way ticket to outer space.

Having said all that, though, I would emphasize something that my father (a police officer) never tired of reminding me of as I was growing up: Ignorance of the law is no excuse. In a negotiating context, what that means is that if you understand the law, you will save yourself, your organization, and your negotiating counterpart a lot of trouble. Just for the record, there are some negotiating rules that I have never, ever found a good reason to ignore. The rule about leaving the Child in the car when you step into someone's world to have a negotiating discussion is a prime example of this kind of rule.

Let me share a true story about a time I pursued negotiations effectively by leaving my Child out of the conversation and communicating instead from my Adult.

My wife Donna and I commissioned a contractor to build a house for us. It wasn't custom designed; we picked the design based on a model home of theirs that we liked. The project stretched over about two years, and during that time I had lots of interactions with the contractor and the various subcontractors.

The most interesting of those interactions began late in the construction, when I visited the site to check in on how things were going. I noticed that the tiles being laid down for our floor weren't the same color we had seen—and chosen—in the model home.

This was a problem. I told the subcontractor about the error, but he said I would have to talk to the contractor. I immediately called the guy who served as my point of contact and told him, too, that the tiles being laid down were the wrong color. He asked for a minute to check his computer, then came back to the phone and told me that

I must be mistaken. His records showed that the right tiles were being used.

Now, this is a potentially stressful situation. I had to take a couple of deep breaths to remind myself not to respond from my Child while I was on the phone with him. My Child would have fixated on who was right and who was wrong. I could have raised my voice, I could have started whining about how unfair that response was, or I could have gotten indignant about the way I was being dismissed and disrespected. But would any of that have helped my cause? Would any of that have moved the negotiation process forward? No.

I ended the call by reminding my contact, firmly but politely, that we had a problem we were going to need to sort out, and that I was counting on him to talk to the subcontractors to confirm that they really did have the right tiles. He said he would. The call ended.

A day later, I went by the construction site, and saw that the subcontractors had finished installing the wrong tiles. Whatever communication was supposed to have happened between my contact and the subcontractors either had not happened or hadn't resulted in any progress in identifying the right tiles to use. Now things got tricky. The subcontractors had finished a major part of the job with the wrong materials. My wife and I faced a choice: Do we just live with the wrong tiles, or do we find some way to get the house we ordered? We wanted the latter choice, but here again, in pursuing that goal, my communicating from my Child wasn't going to get us very far. To the builders, I would just be another customer complaining about something I probably didn't understand. So I started thinking; What would communicating from my Adult look like in this situation?

Well, Adults are all about facts. They're all about the reality on the ground. They don't get swayed by emotion. They're all about determining the actual situation so they can make the best possible decisions, based on the best possible information. I decided to change the dynamic of the conversation by pulling it completely into Adult mode.

I asked the contractor, the subcontractor, and a couple of other people from the builder's side to meet me at the model home my wife and I had looked at. (I knew it was still open.) We all met there and took a look at the color of the tiles. Then we took a short drive over to the construction site and took a look at the color of the tiles there. Lo and behold, everyone agreed on the reality of the situation: The tiles didn't match. We had a problem. We all knew that now. Now that we agreed on that much, we could start working on the solution.

I won't bore you with the details of how the contractor and the subcontractor lost track of what color the tiles in the model home really were. Ultimately, we were provided with the opportunity to pick another tile or another floor all together. Upon reviewing our options, we decided to move away from tile to a new luxury vinyl option. A few days later, the contractor called me and asked if we'd prefer that they tear out the old tile and install the new vinyl, or simply place the new vinyl over the existing new tiles. Two new floors!

I won't pretend that it didn't cost us more because of the increased cost of the luxury vinyl flooring. But I will tell you that we got a substantial break on the cost of putting the right flooring in, and that, most important of all, we got the floor we wanted in our new house—without the drama and acrimony of me complaining about how unfair the world was. By leaving my Child (and, for that matter, my Critical Parent) in the car, I was able to move everyone forward to an outcome that was fair and workable. I never would have gotten to that outcome without an understanding of TA.

Understanding the critical takeaways from TA is, I believe, the first half of mastering the inner game of negotiating. The second half is to be found in an important model known as the Karpman Drama Triangle, which describes dysfunctional communication patterns—something you definitely want to avoid during negotiations.

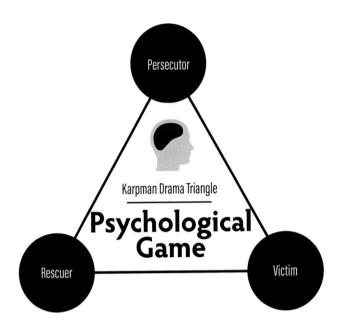

The Drama Triangle

Have you ever been in what felt like a dysfunctional exchange with someone? I thought so—everyone has.

Dysfunctional, as you probably know, is a fancy word for "doesn't work." These stressful communication exchanges that don't accomplish anything often take the form of drama-intense and emotional conversations, discussions, or arguments. They are crisis-heavy, and they are no fun. In 1968, Dr. Stephen Karpman published his work while studying these types of exchanges and summarized them in a model he called the Karpman Drama Triangle.

During a drama-laced or emotional conversation,

people who enter this triangle take on one of three different roles:

1. **The victim:** "Why does everything always happen to me?" The victim's stance is that they cannot do anything about their situation; they believe they are hopeless and unable to work their way out of their problems. They wait for someone to rescue them and pull them out of the hole they are in.

2. **The rescuer:** "Here I am to save the day!" The rescuer needs the feeling that they are helping someone, which allows them to avoid their own negative feelings. "I can help you" is the enabler statement that isn't so much to help the victim as much as to reward the rescuer for their good deeds.

3. **The persecutor:** "Why are you acting that way?" "Why do you always do that?" The persecutor is typically the antagonist in this drama and often plays the "villain" role that initiates the dysfunctional emotional roller coaster.

Here are the two main things you need to know about the Drama Triangle as it relates to negotiation. First, the only way to win this game is not to play. Second, experienced negotiators are going to try to get you to play this game to keep you from thinking rationally. Don't let them.

Conflict Doesn't Have to Be Dysfunctional

When looking at negotiation as a science and breaking down its core skills and competencies, a number of behaviors start to emerge as essential. One thing you will notice is that negotiating, at its most basic level, is all about a person's comfort level with entering conflict.

Those who are low in negotiating competencies will avoid conflict. This could include avoiding certain topics, conversations, and even people. Those who are high in negotiating competencies are comfortable with conflict and don't judge it as good or bad—it is simply a means to an end. They may even believe a discussion that is void of conflict will not uncover the best solution.

If you were able to objectively assess an individual's skill at negotiating, what core behavioral traits would you expect to see? There are five core human behaviors, in addition to negotiating, that when objectively measured indicate if a person will be a strong or weak negotiator. They are: comfort with conflict, assertiveness, competitiveness, ego, and emotional composure.[*]

Those who are uncomfortable with and not open to negotiating come in different types just as those who are comfortable and open do. The uncomfortable ones (low in negotiating skills) are in two basic categories. The first is

---

[*] Source: Outmatch.

obvious: They typically do not negotiate because as a rule they avoid conflict. They see conflict as a negative activity, and they are very low in assertiveness. Because they avoid conflict and are unskilled at navigating it, when they find themselves in a situation where they need to negotiate, others will often experience them as being confrontational or emotional. Key behaviors you will see in these people are low negotiating skills, low comfort with conflict, low assertiveness, low competitiveness, low ego (meaning low in self-esteem and personal confidence), or low emotional composure.

The second category of those who do not like to negotiate is not as obvious because they possess many of the characteristics that people who enjoy negotiating have. They are high in comfort with conflict, high in assertiveness, and high in ego, but still low in negotiating. These people simply have an attitude that "it's my way or the highway." They have no desire to justify, defend, or explain their position, nor are they interested in finding common ground. They want it their way. Period.

Then there are those who are comfortable and very open to negotiating. They come in two categories as well. Some are more moderate in the key negotiating behaviors; others are very high. The former have a balance of expressing their ideas while considering other people's ideas. Although they may have a high strength in one or two of the key behaviors of negotiating, comfort with conflict, assertiveness, competitiveness, ego, and emotional composure, in general they are more moderate in them. This moderation makes them more flexible with others and allows them to adjust to the people involved in the interaction. They are especially effective when they have honed their negotiating skills so that they have a variety of methods to draw from instead of relying on their favorite negotiating tactic. As mentioned, these people can be highly effective; however, if negotiating is a major part of their day-to-day activity, they can become worn out because it is not a natural strength.

Finally there is the category of strong negotiators who are exactly what one would expect. They are very high in most of the key behaviors of negotiating: comfort with conflict, assertiveness, competitiveness, ego, and emotional composure. They enjoy a good debate and may even be guilty of "poking the bear" because when it comes to conflict, they are fearless. However, just as with most characteristics, too much of a good thing is not good. A person who is extremely high in all of these key negotiating behaviors may be deemed by others as pushy, overly aggressive, closed-minded, self-centered, and a host of other unflattering adjectives, especially if they are extremely low in relationship traits. Therefore, self-awareness and other-awareness is key.

You can't deliver quality products and services if you give up too much in the negotiating game. A look into the differing approaches of the amateur negotiator, the tactical negotiator, and the strategic negotiator will help you prepare appropriately for the moves and gambits that are likely to come your way from each. Understanding these three levels will let you know where you are personally and what you need to do to achieve strategic negotiator status. Gaining that level of understanding is the focus of the next three chapters.

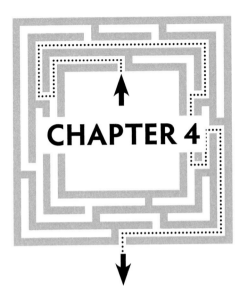

Close-Up on the Amateur Negotiator

L et's start by thinking about how your company buys products and services. Does your company take a process approach to working with their vendors and partners? Or, is the outcome simply up to one individual on your team who is responsible for acquiring what is needed? If the latter is the case, I have another question for you. Is this someone who habitually fixates on only one element of the agreement, such as up-front price?

If that is the case, your company's negotiating efforts are led by an amateur negotiator.

Meet the Amateur Negotiator

Amateur negotiators follow no clear process. They struggle if asked to lay out a step-by-step plan that someone else could follow in negotiating a deal. They often consider themselves to be the negotiating process. They tend to fixate on up-front price.

If this is the individual who handles your company's important negotiations, then your company might be paying more in terms of real costs for solutions than it should. An amateur negotiator who comes on too strong may see elevated turnover in partners and solutions because they are looking for a good deal as opposed to developing a long-term mutually beneficial relationship.

The problem of building your company's negotiating "strategy" (notice the quote marks there) around a single amateur negotiator can be best summarized in a quote from the astronaut and politician John Glenn:

I guess the question I'm asked the most often is: "When you were sitting in that capsule listening to the count-down, how did you feel?" Well, the answer to that one is easy. I felt exactly how you would feel if you were getting ready to launch and knew you were sitting on top of two million parts—all built by the lowest bidder on a government contract.

Here is what you need to know about the amateur negotiator.

They do this part time. The amateur negotiator is typically an occasional negotiator. This person has other professional responsibilities that take up most of the working week and is only occasionally called upon to negotiate a deal.

They will play you against others. They usually have at least three companies vying for their business. They know how to leverage bidders against each other to help determine the "right" solution—which all too often means the solution with the lowest possible price. Of course, this makes you want to determine who your competition is and then ensure you have a strategy to win against those competitors, but this will not always be possible. An important question to ask yourself when negotiating with an amateur negotiator is: If you could get the negotiator to ask a specific set of questions to your competition to help eliminate them, what would those questions be? (Tactical and strategic negotiators may or may not be asking those questions already. Amateur negotiators almost certainly are not.)

They never let you know where you really stand. This

person may be very positive, giving you lots of good feed-back, and may send lots of green-light signals by saying things like, "It looks very good from here." Beware. The amateur negotiator may exhibit that persona to everyone. They may be good at ensuring everyone feels like they are going to win the deal. They may specialize in making you feel you've been able to build a good relationship with them. Unfortunately, as nice as they may seem, they usually aren't nice enough to level with you about where you match up and where you don't. Alternatively, the amateur negotiator may be supremely indifferent to everyone, acting as though everyone in the game is basically the same. They may not be great at relationship building and may be more of a facts-and-figures person. You might be tempted to think that not letting someone know where they stand is not a great way to build a long-term relationship. You'd be right.

They are looking for free consulting. If you'll take the time to educate amateur negotiators, they are more than willing to listen and learn. If you find yourself providing samples, multiple demos, documentation, and (especially!) a free "no commitment" trial, then you should be aware that you are being manipulated. They are using you for your knowledge and, not infrequently, for your willingness to let them try your stuff for free so that they can learn all about it. Salespeople often convince themselves that the more information they provide, the more interested in buying the person they're talking to becomes. Not so. We see this syndrome play out a lot in technology companies, especially ones that have an innovative technology and operate in a market where prospects are not educated on their software or solution. They provide demo after demo and endless 30-, 60-, or 90-day free trials in order to ensure the prospect becomes perfectly educated on their solution. Too many of these people simply never have any intention to buy. They are wasting the salesperson's time, effort, and energy. You may imagine that you are negotiating with them, but you are not. (Side note: A little later in this book, we'll look closely at the important issue of qualification and how it impacts the negotiating process.) Manipulating and using people is not a great way to build a long-term relationship.

They know when to take the deal away (or appear to). These negotiators know that they control the clock, and they know how to use time to their advantage. When they feel it makes sense to them to do so, they will have no problem making you feel like this opportunity is either dead or not a priority for them. They may tell you that time has expired. Sometimes that will be true. Sometimes it won't. Again, not a great relationship-building strategy.

Defending Yourself Against the Amateur Negotiator

There are a couple of areas to address in order to deal effectively with the amateur negotiator. Here's a brief summary of the two most important points to bear in mind.

Be willing to ask some tough, important questions, in a nurturing way. This is an important skill you will want to deploy with any and every negotiator you face, but it is particularly crucial during early discussions with the amateur negotiator. If you want to challenge their paradigm, encourage them to stop treating you and your stuff as commodities, and get them to begin working with you as a partner, you will need to ask tough questions in a way that keeps the conversation moving forward.

One example of an important, tough question you could ask in a nurturing way would be: "Is doing nothing an option?"

This simple yet unconventional, closed-ended question leads the other person to answer yes or no. Closed-ended questions are great, provided you know how to handle both answers. If the person says, "Yes, doing nothing is an option," then you know you are negotiating against change more so than a competitor. If they say no, then you know you're negotiating and selling against competition. You may feel a little uncomfortable asking a question that includes the possibility of the person not working with you. I am here to challenge you to begin asking tough questions anyway. I realize this approach is unconventional, that it may not be what you were expecting. That is OK. Ask tough questions anyway. If doing nothing is a realistic option for the other person, you need to know that going in.

Other examples include: "If you were to move forward with this purchase, when would you need the product/solution up and running? Why then?" If they give you a date, then be sure to ask "why then" so you can ensure there's a good reason that that date must be hit and find out what the repercussions are if that date is not met. This question helps create urgency and a timeline for the project. It also helps you uncover arbitrary deadlines that don't really have any real-world events driving them—except perhaps the negotiator's desire to control the clock.

Another tough question: "I get the feeling that this project may not be a priority. Would you mind sharing with me where this fits within your list of priorities?" This is a great question to ask to avoid the trap of giving away free consulting. Remember this simple rule: Sell today, educate tomorrow.

Create a Monkey's Paw. This powerful strategy, worth considering in any negotiating situation, is particularly effective with amateur negotiators with whom you have not previously worked. It provides a clear structure and gives them an easy path to say yes to a cost-effective option. In the Monkey's Paw scenario, don't overcomplicate the process by introducing lots of additional services or people into the discussion. Instead, ask for a smaller piece of business in order to gain a win and to build trust with the person, instead of going after the entire scope of the work.

By the way, the Monkey's Paw terminology comes from the boating and sailing world. Have you ever seen the large ropes that tie a cruise ship or oil tanker to a dock? These ropes are really big and heavy, so a worker on the boat tosses an attached smaller rope with a ball on the end to the person on the dock. The rope with the ball on the end of it is called a monkey's paw because of the way the knot is tied. The person on the dock then uses that rope to pull the large rope to the dock.

Think of asking for a smaller piece of the business, at first, as being analogous to throwing out that smaller rope. It may be easier for the (ever price-conscious) average buyer to agree to a smaller, less expensive option than the major project that could deliver the entire solution. Getting agreement on that may make it easier for the two of you to work something out in the future.

Let me emphasize that this one best practice can transform your entire negotiating strategy—not just with amateur negotiators (although it is incredibly effective when you are dealing with them) but with all the negotiators you face. I once had a client who sold very large enterprise deals tell me that she received a piece of advice from one of her prospects that totally changed the way she sold enterprise deals: "There is no way a company like mine is going to sign a multi-year, multi-million dollar engagement with a company we've never done business with before. If you want to earn our business, let's find a small project we can work on to ensure we understand how our teams will be able to communicate when we partner on larger projects." My client immediately put that advice to good use.

In the next chapter, we'll take a close look at the tactical negotiator.

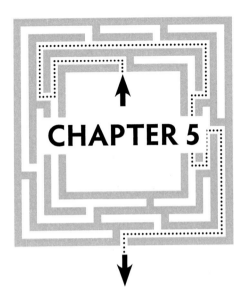

Close-Up on the Tactical Negotiator

The tactical negotiator makes a living buying and negotiating deals for their company. Their formal business title may reflect this professional function in words like "purchasing," "procurement," or "acquisition," and a quick LinkedIn search may be able to tell you whether someone has such a title or has received certification as a Certified Purchasing Manager or a Certified Professional in Supply Management, both of which are a major tipoff. But given the vagaries and unpredictability of the real world, start by accepting that what shows up on this individual's business card may be of little use to you. (Some CEOs, for instance, choose to take on this role within their organization.) Your job is to be able to tell from a person's behaviors when you have run into a tactical negotiator. That's what this chapter will help you do.

It's particularly important to conduct due diligence early on in the relationship, so you can spot those situations where there is a tactical negotiator on the scene and plan your approach accordingly. Bear in mind that if there is someone in the organization who plays this role, you cannot expect to close the deal without engaging with them. You must build them into your process. If you spend a lot of time "negotiating" with an end user who pretends to have final purchasing authority but really doesn't, nobody wins. This suggests again the important question of how to qualify your opportunities, specifically for the decision-making process. This is something we will cover in greater depth in Chapter 9. In the meantime, just remember that asking early on, "Would you mind sharing with me your company's process for buying solutions like these?" will give you the insights you need to prepare appropriately. If there is a formal procurement process, you need to know exactly what it is.

Meet the Tactical Negotiator

Here is what you need to know about the tactical negotiator.

They will avoid engaging. You are likely to receive an email asking you to drop your price, add more products and services, revise your proposal, and send it back. They believe that their best chance of receiving a concession is to not engage in any relationship building and to keep everything electronic.

They are likely to utilize their internal counsel/ lawyers as negotiating allies. If you have ever worked to create a long-term contract with a mid-sized or large organization, it's likely you are familiar with this phenomenon. Throwing lawyers at you changes the dynamic, because attorneys are always working on the principle of self-preservation. The more ruthlessly they can negotiate a contract, without even directly involving the tactical negotiator, the more they prove their worth to the company. Note that the tactical negotiator will usually instruct the lawyers to ask you to sign their contracts instead of them signing yours, which will always give the tactical negotiator's side the advantage.

They may be compensated based on the difference between your proposal price and the final ending price. Naturally, this drives the tactical negotiator to secure the lowest possible up-front price. This dynamic may also create an internal negotiation between the user of the product/solution and the purchasing department, to ensure the user hasn't been "sold" on buying a product/ solution that may not actually solve the problem.

They may assign a separate coach to each of the prospective vendors. These coaches will tell you that they are there to build a relationship with you and help guide you through the process. That's true enough. However, they may also be there to fulfill two important priorities of the tactical negotiator: to ensure they are able to nail down the best deal possible, and to keep you from interacting directly with them. The good news is that they'll negotiate early and often, and they may also let you know where you stand as it relates to what the competition is doing.

Defending Yourself Against the Tactical Negotiator

The more difficult moves this person is likely to throw at you will be covered in later chapters, because they demand a deep analysis and some careful planning if you are to overcome them. In the meantime, here's a brief summary of the most important points to bear in mind when you're dealing with this negotiator.

Early identification of the existence of this person/department is your key. If you know what the decision-making process is, you'll be sure to not negotiate with the user/buyer and will instead hold your negotiable assets and your process until you are dealing with the person who can actually initiate the negotiations and, ultimately, make the decision.

Two can play at the lawyer game. If you find yourself in a situation where the legal team is about to be brought in, your job is actually pretty simple: Ensure you are negotiating as a team and involve your legal counsel as well. Lawyers respect other lawyers and are used to negotiating terms and conditions to a fair point. Believe it or not, this can actually be a positive development for you and your company from a pricing point of view, because lawyers are typically more concerned about reducing risk and finding ways to get out of a contract if they need to than they are about nailing down the lowest possible price. They will want to know the specifics of what you will be delivering and will look for ways to hold you accountable for any negative outcome that may occur with using your company. Work with your legal team and your senior management to come up with the best possible outcomes here.

Make the coach you've been assigned part of your team. Make sure this person is an ally, not an enemy. Remember: They are internally representing you and discussing you and your organization at their internal meetings—you want them to be saying nice things. Treat this coach like one of your team members. Invite them to your office, let them get a feel for your company culture, and expose them to the key people within your company. If you can, and if your senior leadership is amenable to it, get them in front of your CEO/president. Who knows? They may return the favor—or at least get you more face time with the tactical negotiator.

In Chapter 9, I will share a powerful true story about how I turned around the gambit where the strategic negotiator sent an email demanding resubmission of my proposal with a lower price. But there's a lot to cover before we get there.

In the next chapter, let's look at the third, and perhaps most intimidating, category: the strategic negotiator.

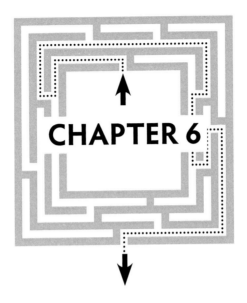

Close-Up on the
Strategic Negotiator

You've seen that the amateur negotiator fixates on price and other short-term outcomes and doesn't mind sabotaging the emerging relationship by manipulating or misleading you. You've also seen that the tactical negotiator tends to build distance in the relationship and likes to leverage institutional assets, such as coaches and attorneys, in generating a deal that works from their point of view. Notice that both of these negotiators don't much care, at least in the early going, whether they create a long-term business relationship with you.

The bad news is that the strategic negotiator has mastered all the classic tricks and strategies of the first two groups of negotiators, and a whole lot of other moves as well. This person may well choose to manipulate you, play you off against other vendors, shut you out, demand major concessions from behind a computer screen, and otherwise mess with your head. In other words, the strategic negotiator may opt to treat you like a commodity when they believe it's in their strategic interests to do so. They have a whole lot of tools at their disposal, more than the other two groups combined. If their goal is to keep you operating at the transactional level, that is, in all likelihood, where you will be operating.

But there is potentially some good news here, too. You can persuade them to change that goal. You can take advantage of the fact that, unlike the amateur or tactical negotiators, this person typically does want to build a relationship with you.

Notice that I have mentioned the word "strategy." The strategic negotiator is far more likely than the other two negotiators to think strategically, on behalf of the long-term best interests of themselves and their organization. That's what makes this negotiator a whole different animal.

Unlike what you face with the other two groups, you typically can create a functional person-to-person relationship with this person, even in the early going. To do that, you must make a plausible, informed, and verifiable case that you can help them achieve their most important strategic goals. While working with the strategic negotiator definitely presents its share of challenges and nasty curveballs, it also presents great opportunity.

Meet the Strategic Negotiator

Here is what you need to know about the strategic negotiator.

They are committed to mastery. This negotiator is a long-term student of the art and science of negotiation. They have turned their knowledge into a calling. They don't just negotiate for a living—they negotiate because they believe the task itself is worth doing better than anyone else. That means they have done more homework, research, and preparation than the amateur and tactical negotiators, and it also means they have more, and more varied, experience than either of those negotiators. You will know them by their long and varied experience, by their high position within the organization they serve, and by the respect they command from others. This is likely a senior executive with many years of service in an industry they know very well indeed.

The strategic negotiator may be a highly charismatic individual, but they didn't get this far just on personality. They have spent a lot of time studying influence, psychology, and business, and of course they have a small library of negotiation books they've devoured. Additionally, they've sought out classes, podcasts, and videos about the subject (they may have read this book already), and they've practiced their negotiating moves intensely, just like a black belt in martial arts would. The strategic negotiator negotiates often, in countless everyday situations. That allows them to strengthen their skills.

They do want to build a relationship with you. Not because they like you (although they may), but because once they know you fairly well they will know what kinds of gambits will work best against you. Ouch. This person knows your DISC style within seconds of meeting you or talking to you on the phone (yes, some people are that good), and will identify potential weak points based on that assessment. They look you up online before they even begin discussions with you. All of this happens because they are always in search of an advantage during negotiations.

They will take you by surprise. I've already mentioned that the strategic negotiator is capable of executing all the tactics that the amateur and tactical negotiators can execute. The big challenge you will face here is that you'll have a much more difficult time seeing those moves coming or preparing for them ahead of time. Time and experience have given the strategic negotiator a lot of advantages, including but not limited to the advantage of surprise. This negotiator has practiced all the moves so often that they have become internalized, and they have executed them so often that deploying them against opponents at the most destabilizing moment has become second nature. Bottom line: You are likely to be thrown off your game. In fact, you may find that you have given up a concession before you even realized that negotiations had begun. That's how good the strategic negotiator is.

They love being the lead negotiator in complex deals. It's possible that you will encounter a strategic negotiator when you are negotiating an opportunity in the enterprise world. These seasoned negotiators are often positioned in the lead role within teams tasked with securing the best terms on projects for large, complex organizations with multiple decision makers. They negotiate in teams and are well connected. They also understand how introducing people at the right time in the process can influence decisions and outcomes—by, for instance, introducing you to the procurement department late in the sales cycle, when they know you are under pressure from your side to wrap things up. Be forewarned that this person not only knows the best negotiating gambits like the back of their hand, but also knows their side's organizational terrain far better than you ever will.

They are patient. One of the most notable traits of the strategic negotiator is their patience. They have a calm presence about them that allows them to be just as strategic in their negotiations as they are tactical. They will not rush things. They will let you do that.

Defending Yourself Against the Strategic Negotiator

Here are the basics when it comes to negotiating with the strategic negotiator.

Salute the flag. You will not outthink, out-plan, or outmaneuver this person, and it's a mistake to imagine you can. Your goal here is to be respectful, avoid even the merest hint of arrogance, and act as though you have a lot to learn from this individual, because you do. That doesn't mean you make instant concessions, but it does mean that you spend your time up front creating an Adult-to-Adult discussion about what the problem that needs solving is, what the costs of that problem are, and what has and hasn't worked in the past. By focusing on asking relevant questions, rather than trying to impress or intimidate the strategic negotiator (neither of which is going to happen), you will increase the odds of presenting yourself as a potential strategic ally.

Do your homework. If there was ever a person you want to google before the meeting, this is that person. Find out as much as you possibly can ahead of time about the strategic negotiator, their organization, and their major challenges. If they've given a speech and it shows up in an online video, watch it. If they've written a white paper, read it. If they've shown up in the news, find out why. Knowledge is power.

Involve them in a team-selling approach to enterprise opportunities. All of the strategic negotiator's tactical, historical, and market experience can either be deployed in support of your pursuit—or in opposition to it. (No prizes for guessing which outcome you want here.) Enterprise deals are not won by winning over one or two decision makers. They are won by building coalitions. Early on in the process, try to match the right person on your team with the right person on the strategic negotiator's team. Get their blessing on all of these assignments, and do so at the outset of the relationship. Strategic negotiators excel at leveraging the strengths of others. See if you can get them to do that collaboratively, with you—and if you can, then follow their lead. This will not mean the strategic negotiator won't throw some nasty negotiating gambits your way. But it will mean that you will be more likely to build a functional working group within the enterprise opportunity.

Build in institutional safeguards, based on past experience with strategic negotiators. These people are going to find ways to win, and yes, some of those victories may come at your expense. If that happens once, so be it. But it doesn't have to happen twice. Learn from the experience, and set up internal structures that make it difficult for the next strategic negotiator to pull the same maneuver. Case in point: One of my clients recently decided to set up an internal "Deal Desk" tasked with reviewing and approving all high-value opportunities before they were agreed to. Basically, this was the "Pushback Desk." My client's management team realized they were discounting too much once they were introduced to a certain buyer's procurement team, which was led by a strategic negotiator. No deal was considered final until the Deal Desk signed off on it—and over time, they secured some significant concessions.

In the next part, we'll look at the heart of the negotiating process I am sharing with you, which I call the Playbook.

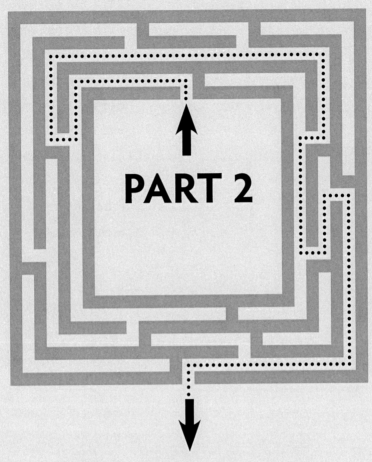

PART 2

The Playbook

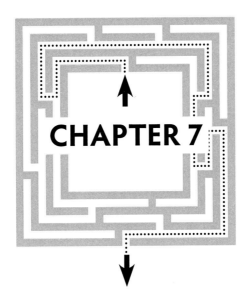

CHAPTER 7

AI, NI, and the Dealmaker's Dozen

Have you ever bought something on Amazon? I bet you have. OK, next question. Have you ever bought something on Amazon that the website somehow "knew" it ought to recommend to you? If you're like most Amazon customers who have been using the service for a while, the answer is yes. So here's a third question for you. How did Amazon know what to suggest?

The answer to that mystery lies in two words that have transformed our world: artificial intelligence. You and I live in an era of artificial intelligence, which is colloquially known as AI. AI has been defined as the study of so-called "intelligent agents": devices capable of perceiving their own environment (which, when you think about it, is a little intimidating) and then taking actions that enhance the possibility of achieving predetermined goals, like making a relevant recommendation to a customer. AI, in other words, allows machines to do much of what we associate with the human activity of thinking. AI is founded on the principle that machines, like people, can recognize patterns in data and can make rapid adjustments based on those patterns.

AI is fascinating and important, but it's a tool. It's something machines do for us. There's something machines can't do, something you can master, something that's even better in my view than delivering an on-target product recommendation to an online customer. In this part of the book, you will begin the process of developing what I call negotiating intelligence, or NI.

Like AI, NI is based on the ability to notice patterns and make rapid adjustments. Once human beings recognize a pattern, though, they face a challenge that machines don't have. They have to understand how to respond emotionally to the situation. I wrote this chapter and the chapter that follows to give you the tools you need to address that problem.

All of this, of course, suggests the concept of emotional intelligence, a topic that could consume ten books this size. I will summarize the key point for you here, though. The more you know about the patterns you are likely to encounter during negotiating discussions, the less stress and confusion you are likely to experience and the better you will be at managing your own emotions as you negotiate.

So let's dive in. There are two critical levels of pattern recognition you need to hone as a professional negotiator.

Pattern Recognition, Level 1: Who Are You Dealing With?

The first and perhaps most important piece of pattern recognition begins with your ability to read the other person. How can you know whether you are looking at a strategic negotiator? This, you'll remember, is someone who negotiates for a living, someone who negotiates well, someone for whom it makes sense for you to invest the time, effort, and energy to prepare and execute a sound negotiating plan before engaging with them. We've already looked at a few of the hallmarks of such an individual, but they're worth reviewing again:

- They hold their information close to the vest.

- They ask you for something very early in your interaction.
- They come prepared, with plenty of research and data, and want to make sure you know that.
- They have ample experience, and want to make sure you know that.

If you see any one of these four signs, you should know that you are very likely dealing with a strategic negotiator. One or more of these signs means this discussion is serious. There are strategic negotiators—and there is everyone else!

You can sometimes get away with improvising when you are dealing with an amateur or tactical negotiator. When you spot a strategic negotiator, winging it is no longer an option. You need a comprehensive strategy. The game is already on, whether you realize it in the early going or not, and you must proceed with deep caution. You need to take the time to prepare for what you are likely to face next when you interact with this person. You must be in a position to manage both your strategy and your emotions intelligently when the strategic negotiator runs a number on you—which they will. The question is, what move will the strategic negotiator make?

This brings us to the next level of pattern recognition you must master.

Pattern Recognition, Level 2: What Are You Likely to Face?

Whenever you enter into a negotiating discussion with a Strategic Negotiator, you are, in all likelihood, going to encounter one or more classic negotiating gambits. These will be deployed craftily, and strategically, and often deceitfully, against you, on the theory that all is fair in love, war, and negotiating. Is that true? Strategic negotiators think so. There are twelve such gambits. Strategic negotiators know them inside and out, and they may opt to use more than one of them against you in a complex, drawn-out negotiating scenario.

I call these twelve gambits the Dealmaker's Dozen. Learning to recognize them in an instant constitutes your next phase of pattern recognition.

Each gambit is a puzzle the professional negotiator must eventually learn to solve. Don't worry about solving them right now. Just focus on recognizing them. I'll show you how to respond constructively to each of the gambits in the following chapters. For now, your job is to begin noticing the patterns.

One great way to do that is to ask yourself which of these twelve gambits have been used against you in the past and what you did in response when it happened. Don't be embarrassed or go into denial about a bad negotiating outcome you experienced. If a particular gambit worked to your disadvantage, admit that that's what happened, and start thinking about why it worked.

Take a look at the list now. Spend some time with this list. On a separate sheet of paper or an electronic device of your choosing, answer the questions that follow each gambit honestly.

#1. Fait Accompli

In the fait accompli gambit, the strategic negotiator simply announces the terms.

This is what happened in the story I shared at the opening of this book, where my counterpart stated his terms, walked out of the room, and left me gaping. It is the brilliant tactic of presuming the deal or negotiations are already done. For instance: You sent the proposal, they made some changes to the terms, rates, warranties, and so on—and then signed on the dotted line and sent it back. Now, you have a signed proposal in hand with terms that you never discussed or agreed to. This happens most often when legal departments are involved.

The key with this gambit, and with all the gambits, is to be aware that it is a gambit. If you're not aware of what just happened, you may make the mistake of beginning to negotiate internally with the sales leadership to try to accept the deal. After all, you have a signed contract in your hands. Hmmm—reverse negotiations! The sales representative starts to negotiate harder internally then they do externally.

Questions:

- Can you think of a time when someone used this gambit on you?
- How did you respond?
- If you're a salesperson, did you ever find yourself trying to get more concessions from your manager than you did from the prospect?
- If you're a sales leader, did you ever find that your salespeople negotiated harder with you than they did with the prospect?

#2. The Best and Final Offer

The strategic negotiator announces something like: "Please just send me a better proposal, and when you do, give me your bottom line. I don't have time to go back and forth. Just get me your best number."

Is this a test? Could be. A smart negotiator is always going to try to get you to negotiate against yourself. This gambit causes you to start thinking about concessions you can give now, so you can present a proposal that proves to the strategic negotiator you've given something because of their request.

Questions:

- Can you think of a time when someone used this gambit on you?
- How did you respond?
- When have you succumbed to pressure to start negotiating against yourself?

#3. The Flinch

When you talk about pricing, the strategic negotiator flinches, says something along the lines of, "Wow, I didn't think it was going to be this much!"—and waits for you to respond.

This gambit happens when a prospect or customer has a slight physical and verbal reaction to your ask, your pricing, or your proposal. No counteroffer. Just a flinch.

This is a very strong move because it can trigger an equal emotional reaction in us, making us feel uncomfortable.

Questions:

- Can you think of a time when someone used this gambit on you?
- How did you respond?
- Have you ever made a concession just to fill an awkward silence in a conversation with a prospect?

#4: "Your Competition Is Cheaper"

The strategic negotiator announces, "We've received a

better price from another provider." Then, they wait for you to do something interesting.

What a great move this is from the prospect! They decided to let you know that you are not the lowest price option. How thoughtful! How compassionate!

If you're not prepared for this, then you're going to fall into the trap of asking where you need to be in order to win the business. And that's not a great response.

Questions:

- ◆ Can you think of a time when someone used this gambit on you?
- ◆ How did you respond?
- ◆ Have you ever asked a prospect, "Where do you need us to be in order for us to win this business?"

#5: Lower/Higher Authority

The strategic negotiator says, "I'm going to have to run this past my _____." (You can fill in the blank yourself here: partner, boss, spouse, whatever.)

By the way, you could have neutralized this possibility entirely if you had performed a good Decision Step[*] as part of your sales process. This includes asking questions like: "When are you going to need the product/services?"

---

[*] For more on the Sandler Selling System steps, check out *You Can't Teach a Kid to Ride a Bike at a Seminar* by David Sandler.

"How do you/how does your company make decisions for services and products like these?" "In addition to you, who else would like to be involved in this process?"

Note that if there is little or no trust in a relationship, you may get inaccurate answers to these questions. Note, too, that very often, people will insist that they can and will make a decision independently, even when they won't. Notice I wrote "won't" there—not "can't."

Questions:

- ◆ Can you think of a time when someone used this gambit on you?
- ◆ How did you respond?
- ◆ Do you always clarify the decision-making process before you make a presentation?

#6. Good Guy, Bad Guy

The strategic negotiator says, "I really like you and your solution, but my _____ doesn't think it's worth it."

Here again, the blank could be partner, boss, spouse, you name it, and the guidance about performing a good Decision Step is just as relevant.

This gambit may well be the oldest one in the book. When it's used effectively, it causes you to feel like the bad guy doesn't like you. If you have a high need for approval, then you'll move straight to concessions in order to get the deal done.

Questions:

- Can you think of a time when someone used this gambit on you?
- How did you respond?
- Is it possible a need for approval may have affected your negotiating discussions in the past? If so, how?

#7: Hot Potato

The strategic negotiator says something like, "Our budget for this project was just reduced by 20%," then waits for you to respond.

Translation: "Rescue me!" Your superhero button just got pushed.

Will you put on your cape and save the day? The pressure to do so can seem overwhelming. You're a problem solver, right? But notice: Once you decide to get suited up, you have a problem—and they don't!

Questions:

- Can you think of a time when someone used this gambit on you?
- How did you respond?
- Has there ever been a negotiating discussion where the prospect presented you with a problem that had (supposedly) arisen in their world, and you felt pressure to solve that problem?

#8. The Emotional Outburst

The strategic negotiator looks agitated, loses their cool, and shouts something like, "There's no way we are going to be able to do that!" (This may be accompanied by flailing arms and swear words.)

Very few people enjoy it when someone else expresses anger toward them, which is why this gambit works so well, so often. It can make you feel like a child who just got scolded and sent to their room.

But guess what? More often than you suspect, this person is not angry at all. For the strategic negotiator, this is a consciously deployed strategy. It's an act. Beneath the surface, the strategic negotiator is cool as a cucumber.

Questions:

- Can you think of a time when someone used this gambit on you?
- How did you respond?
- Have you ever made a concession impulsively when a prospect expressed anger or other negative emotions?

#9. Stonewalling

You seem to be getting somewhere, but after an apparently good discussion, the strategic negotiator simply stops communicating and vanishes from the radar screen, with no explanation.

Stonewalling is a consciously imposed period of silence following a meeting or discussion. Suddenly there's no communication. You're ghosted. The building has gone dark.

When communication ceases in this way, it is because the strategic negotiator has the aim of enticing you to come back to the table with a better offer—say, a month-end or year-end discount—as the price for getting them to re-engage with you.

Questions:

- Can you think of a time when someone used this gambit on you?
- How did you respond?
- Sometimes people fall out of touch because they are busy, and sometimes people fall out of touch on purpose. Can you think of a specific buyer who may be using falling out of touch as a negotiating tactic?

#10. Changing the Cast of Characters

You seem to be making progress, but then you learn there's an unexpected personnel change that you have to deal with. The strategic negotiator announces, "I'm going to be handing this project over to my replacement, so you can work out the final details with them."

What? Who? In comes a new person with a new perspective, someone you have no rapport with and who hasn't been emotionally involved in the discussion.

Since no mutual trust has been built up with this new person, they have no problem changing the rules of the game, and you find yourself with very little (or no) leverage.

Questions:

- Can you think of a time when someone used this gambit on you?
- How did you respond?
- How do you feel when you are transferred from one customer service person to a different one and must explain the entire situation all over from scratch to the new person? Why do you think a prospect would choose to put you through basically the same kind of experience in a negotiating situation?

#11. Nibbling

Early in the discussion, the strategic negotiator gives you one or more seemingly minor requests and offers nothing in return. For instance: "Will you be able to throw a few extra licenses in for me?" Or: "Can I get these upgrades at last year's price?"

When someone negotiates in this way, you can start to feel like they are leaning in, that they want to do business.

Hey, at least they're engaging with you. They asked for something! Of course, you'd like to give them what they've asked for.

Typically, this gambit plays out before you have even talked about the budget. It's a pre-emptive strike.

Questions:

+ Can you think of a time when someone used this gambit on you?
+ How did you respond?
+ Who in your current customer/prospect base is the worst "nibbler"?

#12. Promise of Escalation

The strategic negotiator says something like, "We have a whole lot of business we're going to be sending your way, so give us a great deal on this first one."

The idea here is to make you feel compelled to do a skinny deal because you want to get your foot in the door. It's also known as the quantity gambit.

Surprise, surprise: You can never go back to a higher pricing or margin model once they know you have the ability to do a deal at a lower rate.

Questions:

+ Can you think of a time when someone used this gambit on you?

- How did you respond?
- In your experience, has a client or customer ever responded positively when asked to pay more for the same product or service?

Before moving on, let me challenge you to think closely about the opportunities you've worked through over the past year. Spend some time documenting how those people negotiated. Which gambits did they use most often? What words did they use to execute a given gambit? This exercise is all part of mastering pattern recognition, which is the essential first step.

Now What?

These, then, are the Dealmaker's Dozen. Each and every one of these gambits has the capacity to finalize the deal to your disadvantage. That's why strategic negotiators use them. So, how can you keep from falling victim to them?

Recognize them for what they really are, so that you are emotionally prepared for them when they do show up. (Which they will.)

Set up a strategy that neutralizes them. The next two chapters give step-by-step instructions on how to do that.

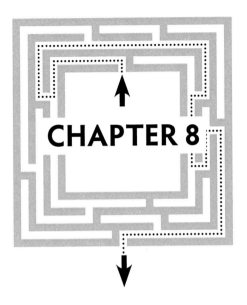

CHAPTER 8

The Master Playbook/ Fait Accompli

I f you're like most of the people I work with, you read the list of the Dealmaker's Dozen and felt a mixture of frustration and relief. The frustration may have been from realizing how much you lost when one or more of these gambits were used on you. The relief may have arisen when you understood, perhaps for the first time, that these were gambits that were being used to manipulate you and take advantage of you. That is an essential insight. The question now becomes not whether you feel good or bad about yourself, not whether you are confused and dis-oriented by something you didn't see coming, but what strategy you can use in response when you run into one of these moves and your pattern recognition kicks in.

No one idea can address every negotiating challenge, but the three-step process I'll be sharing with you in this chapter, which I call the master playbook, comes pretty close. The master playbook is your first line of defense. Choosing whether and how to apply it to your negotiating situation will be your first critical decision point. It is the heart of the negotiating system I am sharing with you.

Think about anything that works really well within your company or your life. I believe you'll find that things that work consistently, time and time again, work as the result of a system. When you turn on your computer, does it give you access to the tools you need? A system supports that. Do you get up every morning, initiate the same routine, and start work more or less when you are supposed to? A system supports that. Even improv comedy performers work based on a system. The result may seem spontane-ous, and in the moment it is, but a guiding set of principles delivers the positive outcome. That is how a system works.

Most systems work because they've been well thought out, tested, and can take over when a person needs them to. The three-step master playbook is such a system. It applies directly or indirectly to every negotiating situation. You may want to make it your first stop in determining the answer to an important question: "How should I respond when I know the other person is running a negotiating gambit against me?"

The master playbook is definitely a system worth practicing and mastering. It has three simple steps.

Step 1: ARA (Acknowledge, Reassure, and Ask). You acknowledge what the person has just said to you, reassure them that your product/service/solution is going to resolve their problem, and ask a question that moves the conversation back to them.

Step 2: Struggle and Redirect. This is a psychological move in which you purposely make the other person feel like they are putting undue pressure on you, and then move away from the possibility of identifying a positive outcome together. This strategic redirection is a tactic; its purpose is to point the conversation in a whole different direction, a direction of your choosing. Yes, this takes practice to execute properly. If you've ever heard that sales is acting, well, you're right. So is negotiation.

Step 3: Concessions (Give Something to Get Something). In other words, make a concession in order to get a concession. Concessions may mean moving away from or adding to your original position, proposal, or offer in order to move a deal forward or finalize it. If you do that, you can ask the other person to do so also in exchange for you making the concession. Never offer concessions unilaterally.

The process you've just read is your first step in determining the answer to the all-important question "How should I respond?" It's the foundation of a negotiating system that actually works—a powerful, broadly applicable template for an Adult response when a strategic negotiator tries to pull a gambit on you. Let's see how this plays out in relation to the first of our negotiating gambits, the Fait Accompli.

#1. Fait Accompli

In the fait accompli gambit, the strategic negotiator simply announces the terms.

Remember the story I told at the beginning of this book? My negotiating counterpart simply announced to me that the terms of the payment for our invoicing error would be X, saw that I had frozen in fear, and stalked out of the room in triumph. What if, instead of freezing in fear, I had said:

Step 1: ARA (Acknowledge, Reassure, Ask): "I can certainly understand your frustration. This issue has been dragging on a long time due to our error. If I were in your shoes, I would feel the same way. But can I ask you one thing before you go?" (Notice that this is an Adult-to-Adult response to the tactic, delivered without fear or anxiety, one that makes it much harder for someone to simply leave the room.)

Assume that at that point, they say, "What's that?"

Step 2: Struggle and Redirect. What if I then said, "Well, frankly, you're putting us under a lot of pressure here. The way things stand now, I don't know when or if I'd be able to get authorization for any amount if we can't at least come to terms on what the major issues are. So here's my question. We've got an hour scheduled for this meeting. We've only used about five minutes of it. Would it make sense to spend twenty minutes now going over what we've learned on our side, and then spend another twenty minutes talking about where you think we might go from here? Because if we don't at least do that, my CEO won't sign off." (If you've been paying attention, you'll notice that I'm running a gambit of my own here, a variation on lower/higher authority. Again: Negotiation is acting.)

Step 3: Concessions (Give Something to Get Something). Now that we've got a conversation going, my negotiating partner might say something like this: "Look, I've spent way more time on this invoicing problem than I want to. It is not a problem we created. But I take your point. Still—I've got a busy day. I'll give you ten minutes to make your case. We'll see where it goes from there." Progress! I could respond to that by saying,

"I appreciate that, but I do think we're going to need a little more than ten minutes to get anything constructive accomplished today. Suppose we gave ourselves half an hour, and then made a decision at that point about what needs to happen next?" And suppose he nodded and we got down to business.

Is this the entire negotiation? Of course not. Is it the template for a constructive negotiation conversation? Absolutely. I would continue to follow the three steps, flexibly but strategically, as the conversation moved forward.

What about the situation where you sent out the proposal, they made some changes to the terms, rates, warranties, and so on, and then signed on the dotted line and sent it back to you via email? How does the master playbook apply in that situation? You're not face-to-face with the client, so you're only going to try to execute the first step of the playbook. Take a look.

Step 1: ARA (Acknowledge, Reassure, Ask): In a response email, write, "Thank you for sending over the contract; I really appreciate your taking the time to review it closely. I would do the same if I were in your position. Can I ask you something, though? It appears that there are a few areas we need to discuss before we finalize and countersign the engagement. Can we set aside 15 minutes on the phone for the two of us to walk through the engagement together so we can resolve this quickly and get this project started?"

When you aren't face-to-face, sometimes the first step is all you need. Remember what I said earlier about the master playbook applying directly or indirectly to all negotiating situations? Here, you have the objective of getting the person on the phone, so you can review the changes point by point. Nine times out of ten, an email message based on ARA will do just that. Once you are on the phone, you will use the full, three-step master playbook to address each and every outstanding issue that is keeping you from closing the deal.

Why wouldn't you take this approach? Isn't it better than rushing to your sales manager and negotiating with them? There is an essential selling and negotiating principle to take into account here: You can't lose what you don't have. At this point, you don't have a valid contract or a sale, so how could you lose it? What do you have? The willingness of the prospect to engage. They want your product or solution, otherwise they would have never signed the contract in the first place.

It Works!

The simple three-step process I have shared with you in this chapter is the basic road map for Adult negotiating conversations, even if you are dealing with a strategic negotiator.

I've shown you how it applies to the first gambit, the Fait Accompli. In the next chapters, I'll show you how it applies to the other eleven.

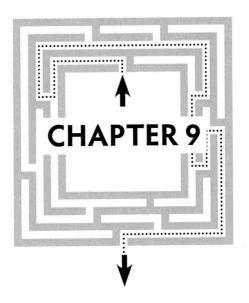

CHAPTER 9

The Best and Final Offer

The best and final offer gambit of the Dealmaker's Dozen is when the strategic negotiator announces something like: "Please just send me a better proposal, and when you do, give me your bottom line. I don't have time to go back and forth. Just get me your best number."

I have told you that the master playbook is like a roadmap. Just as you would with a roadmap you use on a physical journey, you will sometimes use this roadmap to negotiate a hasty detour when you encounter an unexpected roadblock. That's going to be your approach when you encounter a best and final offer gambit. You're going to use only the first of the three steps, and when you do, you're going to pull back and simply hit pause on the negotiating process. You're going to hang back until you identify a route around the roadblock. You're not going to give in to the demand to make concessions, but you're not going to raise the temperature in the relationship, either.

There are two dimensions that you need to master for the second gambit: the immediate response and the underlying problem. The first dimension, the short-term response, is simplest. We'll cover that first.

The Immediate Response

These days, it is common to receive a best and final offer gambit digitally, by means of an email or text message. In fact, this is how strategic negotiators like to operate. There are fewer variables they have to take into account, and a certain percentage of (weak) negotiators will capitulate instantly, granting major concessions right away because they feel they must either respond obediently to the command they've just read—or lose the deal. There is a third way. It begins with the first step of the playbook. Here it is again:

Step 1: ARA (Acknowledge, Reassure, and Ask). You acknowledge what the person has just said to you, reassure them that your product/service/solution is going to resolve their problem, and ask a question that moves the conversation back to them.

Let me share a story that illustrates exactly how this works. One of my training engagements began with me dealing with a senior director of sales training and enablement with an international hospitality media company. I'll call him Rickie. Over a 90-day sales cycle, Rickie and I co-created a proposal. As I went over an advanced draft of it with him, I knew he still had to have our proposal approved by Lynne, the EVP of Sales, with whom I'd previously had several conversations. Rickie told me everything looked good on the proposal. We were scheduled to speak with Lynne a few days later. Then suddenly, out of the blue, I received an email from Rickie asking me to resubmit the proposal with a lower price.

This was the first "poke" at my proposal, and it came via email. My response was simple: "Sounds like we need to talk. Let's chat today at 3:00 p.m." His response? Simple as well: "No need to talk. Please resubmit your revised proposal." Now what?

My next response was straight from our playbook, the first of our three steps: "I appreciate you asking for a revised proposal, and I am glad you are sharing all this with me. I can assure you that based upon our discussions and the deliverables you and I created to train your teams, the investment we discussed is necessary to provide the training to develop your teams. Can we schedule a phone meeting?"

I hit "send," but I was really hitting "pause." I waited to see what happened next. I did not simply cut my price by 10%, or any percentage, nor did I continue the negotiation process via email message. My point here is that you have to have a process and system to follow. I eventually got that voice-to-voice call, and I got it because I followed a process. If I hadn't scheduled and held that call, I don't believe I would have ever won that opportunity. Oh, and by the way, once I started training their sales team, Rickie would reference our negotiation's email and verbal conversations to make a point to his team that they need to know this process.

The key to crafting an effective immediate response to a best and final offer gambit is to understand that it is a gambit. It's a chess move designed to provoke a weaker move from an opponent. Although this gambit is usually presented as the end of a conversation, it usually signals the beginning of one.

The Underlying Problem

There is a deeper issue to consider here, and it has to do with your sales process. When a strategic negotiator uses this gambit against you, it can only be successful if you have been flying blind. In other words, if you have not fully qualified the opportunity. By qualify, I mean:

- Identify the specific business problem, or **pain**, that you can solve or how high the costs (emotional, financial, political, or logistical) are for the other person if they leave that problem unsolved. If you don't know that, you have very little leverage when it comes to responding to any threat from the strategic negotiator to simply walk away from the discussions. You don't know whether living with the pain or taking another approach to addressing it is a viable option. In the true story I just told you, I had spent three months with Rickie identifying the pain he was experiencing and its real-world implications for his company.

- Identify their **budget**. There needs to be a frank discussion about how much they are willing to invest to solve the problem that has been identified. That discussion needs to happen before you submit a formal proposal or recommendation. In my negotiation with Rickie, he and I had discussed budget in depth before I sent in my proposal. I eventually had to do some horse trading to get a package that worked for both sides, but notice that that discussion grew out of our earlier discussions about budget. I had a broad sense of what would work in terms of investment. If I had had no idea what he and his company were willing to pay, I would have been far more vulnerable to his gambit.

- ◆ Identify the **decision-making process.** I can't tell you how many companies I work with whose status quo is simply sending in a proposal that has had zero engagement from the other side, with zero sense of what will happen next. This is the "email and follow up" school of selling and negotiation. It equates to begging for the strategic negotiator to use this gambit against you—successfully. It doesn't have to be that way. Asking early on, "Would you mind sharing with me what your company's process is for buying solutions like these?" will give you the insights you need to prepare appropriately. Notice that, in the story I just shared, I had a clear sense of what would happen next when I sent in my proposal: Rickie and I would discuss it with Lynne. After the failed gambit, that's exactly what happened.

To defend yourself effectively against the best and final offer gambit (and all the other gambits, for that matter), you must qualify the opportunity. That means you must complete a pain discussion, a discussion about the budget, and a discussion about the decision-making process. Don't send in a proposal until you have done these three things. This needs to become second nature.

Is refusing to send in a proposal to an unqualified lead what you are most familiar with? Maybe not. Is it what other people will want you to do all the time? No. Are you going to do it anyway? Yes.

Recently, I got to the point with a law firm prospect in which I was going to provide the proposed deliverable. I had asked for a date and time for us to review it through our video conferencing system. The managing partner asked if I would email it to them. Then, they would get back to me. This is a common request for me, and I am guessing it is one you get a lot, too. It was also the beginning of the negotiation phase with this client, even though it might not have looked like that.

I responded by saying, "I don't do that. I like to ensure everything we discussed is accurate the first time. Most of the time, there are questions about the deliverables that we can address as we're reviewing the proposal together. So, when do you have 15 minutes for us to go through this?" When that phone appointment time came, I emailed him the proposal so we could walk through it together. The phone was the best available option for meeting, and I took it. I would have much preferred a video conference because it gives me the chance to read the other person's body language, listen to any concerns, and ensure I am crafting a proposal that is 100% accurate to expectations. But I took the call, and it inoculated me against later problems (like a best and final offer gambit).

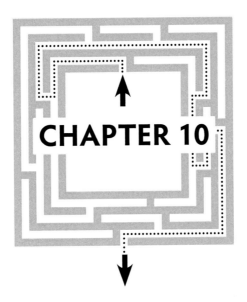

CHAPTER 10

The Flinch

The flinch gambit of the Dealmaker's Dozen looks like this: When you talk about pricing, the strategic negotiator flinches, says something along the lines of, "Wow, I didn't think it was going to be this much!"—and waits for you to respond.

When the strategic negotiator sends out a slight, seemingly involuntary physical or verbal reaction to your ask, your pricing, or your proposal, you've been flinched. I say "seemingly" because in fact the reaction is in fact quite intentional. When executed properly, the flinch is extremely effective, because it causes the other person to experience emotional turmoil—assuming that person is not a strategic negotiator. If the person on the receiving end of the flinch is a strategic negotiator, there's no emotional turmoil. Everyone in the room understands that this is a tactic.

Perhaps the most important thing to understand about this particular gambit is that it is almost always used at the beginning of the negotiating phase. No matter what the other person says, implies, or uses their body language to convey, the odds are good that this is the beginning, not the end, of your discussion about price—or whatever it was they flinched about. Treat it as such. If negotiation is like a chess game—and very often, it is—then this is the opening move, not checkmate. Unless, of course, you opt to treat it as checkmate, which you are certainly not going to do.

Here's another negotiating rule for you: "Only the prospect can become emotionally involved." It means that, in a truly professional selling and negotiating cycle, you need to remain emotionally disengaged, even if the other person seems to be having a strong emotional reaction. Never let your emotions dictate what you say or do. Whenever there is an emotional moment from the other side, you need to have zero emotional reaction. Your response, if you choose to make any, has to be nonemotional and supremely logical. We call this staying in the Adult state, in keeping with the TA model in Chapter 3.

NEGOTIATING RULE

Only the prospect can become
emotionally involved.

Since this gambit is typically used on price, it should go without saying that you can eliminate it or minimize its impact by doing a solid Budget Step in the qualification process you learned about in Chapter 9. Before you provide pricing and a proposal, be sure that you've discussed the investment levels your prospect is willing and able to make for a product/solution/service like yours to solve their concerns.

Truth be told, however, you will occasionally run into strategic negotiators who will find (or manufacture) some reason to use the flinch on you, even though you have already discussed pricing. For instance, they may pretend that you didn't mention payment terms, and then flinch when they read the part of the proposal that points out that your terms are net 30 days. When you find yourself in such a situation, you will want to consider adapting the master playbook to the situation. Following are some ideas on how you could do that.

Step 1: ARA (Acknowledge, Reassure, and Ask). "I can tell by your reaction that this was a little bit of a surprise, and that's OK. You might have been expecting something different. Am I right about that?" The other person will respond in the affirmative and give you some details. This is good, because you want to start some back and forth.

Step 2: Struggle and Redirect. After any response from the strategic negotiator that implies you've sprung something surprising and unfair, consider saying something like the following: "I hear what you're saying, but frankly, I am struggling a little bit here. I can assure you that based on what you and I have talked about, this price really is what we are looking at if we want to address the issues you've got. It seems to me, based on your reaction, that you might have been looking for something different. We might not be right for you. Maybe we need to go back and take another look at the problem you're trying to solve."

Notice that you are now suggesting a discussion about whether the two of you got the problem right, not whether the solution (or its pricing) needs to change. (Save that for the concessions step.)

If you've done your job up to this point, the other

person will acknowledge, in some form or fashion, that you have in fact identified the right problem. It's just possible, though, that they will still insist that what you've just "sprung" on them is somehow a violation of what they had been led to expect. Don't get into a debate about that. Move on to Step 3.

Step 3: Concessions (Give Something to Get Something). "OK, well, given that we're looking at the right problem, let's see whether we can scale back what we're doing, so we can find a way to match your expectations." What you suggest next really shouldn't be a dramatic, unilateral slashing of your pricing. Instead, change the proposal. For instance: If it was big, make it smaller. If it was already small, make it tiny. Or, add in something of value to the proposal that will enhance your offerings and solution, rather than diminish it. Do not alter your pricing, or anything else, without changing what you are proposing to deliver.

You may end up boiling your proposal down to a miniature version, so as to make an initial engagement easier for the other person to agree to. Then again, you may get your negotiating partner to move a step closer to acknowledging reality—by either agreeing to your terms or making a credible counteroffer. Remember, a dialogue between adults is what you're after here. I can tell you from personal experience that that dialogue is much more likely to happen when the other person sees that you understand the flinch for what it is—a gambit—and accepts that you're not simply going to slash prices based on a need for their approval.

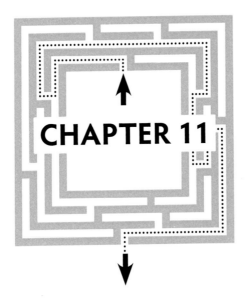

"Your Competition Is Cheaper"

Here's what the negotiating gambit of "your competition is cheaper" will probably sound like:

- "Just so you know, your competition is coming in a little bit lower."
- "I should probably tell you that we've received a better price from another provider."

- "You're not the only bidder on this, and so far you are not the lowest, either."

I do hope you were not assuming you were going to be the lowest-priced option. That would be a strange opening assumption.

If you're not prepared for this gambit, then you're going to fall into the trap of asking where you need to be in order to win the business. Or, even worse, is the knee-jerk reaction to respond with, "Well, let's take a look at our solution to see what we can remove from our solution to bring the price down." That's what the strategic negotiator wants you to do. But if you follow the playbook, you can point the conversation in a whole different direction.

Step 1: ARA (Acknowledge, Reassure, and Ask). "I can assure you that that's not unusual. We know we aren't the bottom of the line option. Do you mind if I ask you something about that, though?" The strategic negotiator will respond in the affirmative. (Just about everyone will, for that matter.)

Here is an alternate approach: "Thank you for sharing that with me. I do appreciate that you gave me the heads up. I can assure you that based upon the situation you have, our solution is going to solve issues [X, Y, Z] that you're having. I'm curious though, what do you prefer about our solution over the others that you've received?"

NEGOTIATING RULE

Get mentally and emotionally tough.

And here is a particularly powerful variation: "Interesting, and I'm glad you mentioned that—but I am wondering about something that maybe you can help me out with. Since they have a lower price point, can you share with me what that means as it relates to how they value their solution? Why do you think they value their offering at that level?"

Step 2: Struggle and Redirect. "I have to say that I'm a little bit surprised that you brought that up, because I didn't think a bottom-of-the-line option was what you were looking for. But if that's the case, then it's possible what we're offering might not be right for you. I'm getting the feeling that you probably like their solution better. Am I right about that?"

This approach reflects another important negotiating rule: "Get mentally and emotionally tough." This classic redirect is an example of doing that. You must act like you are not thrown by what you have just heard (even if you are) and proceed directly to the next phase of the conversation by directly raising the possibility of not working together if price is the only criterion. (Reality check: Do you really want to be in a business relationship with someone where price is the only criterion? I didn't think so.)

Bottom line: It's not your job to justify the higher price. Get them to justify the lower price.

Following either of those approaches, you will probably want to share a third-party story that illustrates the perils of working with a low-end provider. The idea here is to use social proof to land the point that picking the lowest bidder often backfires. Don't make the attack yourself, but do share the experiences of someone else who had a negative experience as the result of fixating solely on price.

Step 3: Concessions (Give Something to Get Something). "Let's pretend our pricing was exactly the same as our competitors. Who would you choose?" This question will open up the conversation a little bit, and perhaps even help you and the strategic negotiator to focus directly on the value you are hoping to deliver. Continue with: "What if we threw in five more licenses?" Or: an extended service plan. Or anything else that adds perceived value to the package without you lowering your price. You don't want to volunteer to cut your price, but you may want to add something of value. This gives the strategic negotiator something to point to when discussing the deal with others, something that can be used to justify the decision to go with you: "Yes, we're paying X, but now we're getting Y as part of the package."

A few thoughts on value positioning are in order before we move on. By the way, what I am about to share is relevant to every discussion you may have about pricing, not just the "your competition is cheaper" gambit.

There are really only three ways you can differentiate yourself from your competition:

1. **Your sales/engagement process.** Begin here, because this process needs to be dramatically different than what they experience from your competitors. Prospects have to see and come to believe that interacting with you is a totally different experience than interacting with the competition. People will not judge you as better until they see you as different.

2. **The uniqueness of your solution to their problems.** This is really the promised land. If your solution is utterly unique, then you really have no competition. The way to get to this point is to be extremely diligent with your questions and exploration of their situation. The more you understand about them and their problems, the more you'll be able to customize a deliverable that cannot be duplicated by your competition.

3. **Service delivery.** If your product or service is not all that different, then you have to focus on differentiating the ways you deliver your customer experience.

Your ability to provide a unique and different way of delivering a commodity product or service can prove to be a slight edge. Think Starbucks. I know a lot of people may argue that their coffee is quantitatively better than that of competing outlets, but that's debatable. I believe the real reason for their dominance is the experience they create with the environment in which consumers interact with them. The delivery experience they have carefully designed and consistently execute allows them to charge a premium price for something that used to be considered a commodity: a cup of coffee.

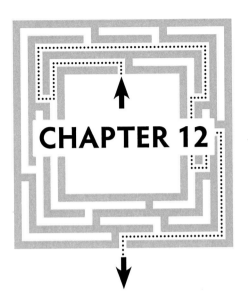

CHAPTER 12

Lower/Higher
Authority

I n the lower/higher authority gambit, the strategic
negotiator tells you something like, "I'm going to have
to run this past my _____." (You can fill in the
blank yourself here: partner, boss, spouse, whatever.)

Note that you would not have been vulnerable to
this gambit if you had performed a good Decision Step
by asking questions like: "When are you going to need
the product/services?" "How do you/your company
make decisions for services and products like these?" "In

addition to you, who else would like to be involved in this process?"

Fortunately, this issue is relatively straightforward. If you do find yourself dealing with this gambit, here's how you can repair the damage and get your process back on track.

Step 1: ARA (Acknowledge, Reassure, and Ask). "I appreciate that, I will probably have to run this past my [authority figure] as well. By the way, often in this situation, typically what ends up happening is the [authority figure] puts it back on you. If they do put it back to you, what would you say? You want to be prepared for that."

Step 2: Struggle and Redirect. "I should probably tell you, though, that I am struggling a little bit with where you stand on this. Let's pretend [authority figure] says no or tells you it is time for you to suggest something. What are you going to do? Is this something you want to hang your hat on?" If there is more pushback, say something like, "Let's back up. Maybe you're right; maybe this isn't the right option for you. You clearly have mixed feelings on it, and if you take this to your boss and they have mixed feelings on it, maybe it's not in the cards. Are we done here?"

Note that you may be dealing with someone who isn't the decision maker—but who may be responsible for creating a short list of suppliers. Asking "Are we done here?"

basically gives them the incentive to tell you what they need in order to move the idea up the chain. It also gives you a better sense of who's actually doing what. If you have done the Pain and Decision Steps properly, what you should hear here is, "No, no, I do want to make this work." If you don't hear that, it's a sign that you may have missed something.

You can do the Decision Step properly and still have the result be that you're going to be dealing with a committee, one that isn't open to meeting with you directly. That's life. The difference is, you want your contact acting as your advocate in dealing with that committee. You want your contact to be transparent with you about what is necessary to win the committee over. If your contact isn't prepared to take up your cause and debate on your behalf with their own boss, you need to know that up front. What will happen if the boss is unsure or against it?

Step 3: Concessions (Give Something to Get Something). Instead of closing on the deal, close on the next step, ideally in a way that expands your contact base. You can say, "How about this? Take this to your boss, and if there is support, great, then we go forward. But if not, let's talk for 30 minutes on Wednesday—you, me, and your boss. Can we set up that slot on your calendar, so we can debrief and figure out where we go from there?"

NEGOTIATING RULE

Only decision makers can get
others to make decisions.

It is extremely important to resist the urge to negotiate concessions with someone who can't say yes. Bear in mind that a strategic negotiator will instruct someone else to use this gambit—using your point of contact within the organization to secure concessions, knowing that that person will be able to get, but not give. Don't let that happen. Strive for direct access. Do not negotiate concessions with messengers.

Of course, it is entirely possible that you won't receive a commitment to get the boss (or the committee, or whoever) on the line for the next call. If that's the situation you face, just schedule the call between you and the contact. But do make the effort to expand your contact base within the organization.

This brings us to another negotiating rule: "Only decision makers can get others to make decisions."

You need to be ready to make a decision to move on when it is appropriate. Your ability to help people decide yes or no will help you work through this gambit.

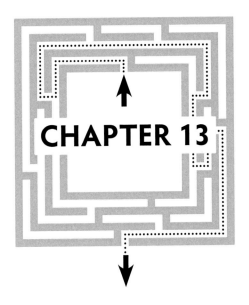

Good Guy, Bad Guy

n the classic good guy, bad guy gambit, you hear something like, "I really like you and your solution, but my _____ doesn't think it's worth it."

This manipulative ploy is meant to make you feel as though the hypothetical "bad guy" doesn't like you. How can you possibly fix that? If you have a high need for approval, you'd move straight to concessions to get the deal done and make sure everyone thinks you're wonderful.

Instead, when you encounter this gambit, I want you to stop and think: How would a strategic negotiator respond to this? Would that negotiator simply disintegrate and ask, "OK, what do we need to do to make your person happy?" Of course not. It's far more likely the strategic negotiator would say something like the following.

Step 1: ARA (Acknowledge, Reassure, and Ask). "OK—I get it. [Name] is not on board with this. Thanks for sharing that with me, and I understand that that puts you in an awkward position. Just out of curiosity—is there any one part of what we worked on that [name] has a problem with, or is it the whole idea of us working together?" At this point, your negotiating partner will probably say something like, "[Name] just felt the price was too high." You can then move on to Step 2.

Step 2: Struggle and Redirect. The right response to this gambit is always to do what we call "going for the no." Step 2 is when you move slightly away from the prospect. That allows you to let the good guy and bad guy fight it out between themselves if necessary.

You might say, "I hear you. But I'm really at a loss with how to move forward. Let me ask you this. If we just stopped here and didn't do anything, is that OK? Is doing nothing an option?" If you've done your job properly up to this point, the other person will acknowledge that they do want to move forward, but they need some incentives to make the "bad guy"—the partner or whoever—feel better about the deal.

Another powerful variation on Step 2 might sound like this: "I make it a practice not to work with a divided house, so if you two are not on the same page and 100% committed then it's probably best if we don't move forward." The transition to Step 3 would then go something like: "So let's do this: Let's find a time for the three of us to sit down and work this through together. At the end of that time, if we're still in the same situation, then we'll know we made a good decision not to move forward. Make sense?"

This, by the way, is called Negative Reverse Selling®. It is not a difficult concept to understand, but is sometimes a difficult process to apply at first, because it means doing something that is unnatural to what you've been taught: step away from the desire to please others. You're doing the opposite of what prospects expect you to do.

Depending on the response to what you've put forth in Step 2, you could then move on to Step 3.

Step 3: Concessions (Give Something to Get Something). "What if we found a way to think outside the box about this? What if we added something to the solution that would make [name] feel more positively about moving forward? I know the dollars and cents are important, but what do you think they value even more than that, that would help us to move this across the finish line?" The aim here is to start a conversation about some add-on, such as additional licenses or different payment terms, that will help you to close the deal.

By using this slight pull away strategy, you place the good guy in the position of having to do the mental exercise of themselves selling the bad guy on the idea of moving forward. Doesn't that make more sense than you having to do it—especially when you consider that the whole issue of the bad guy's disapproval is, in all likelihood, a tactic by the good guy?

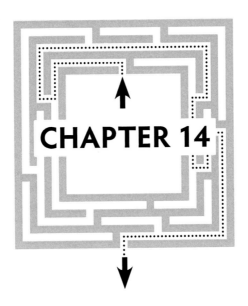

Hot Potato

In the hot potato gambit, the strategic negotiator says something like, "Our budget for this project was just reduced by 20%," then waits for you to throw it back to them with a response. Translation: "Rescue me!" Your willingness-to-help button just got pushed.

If you play the game you're being asked to play, you're at a disadvantage. Suddenly you're a problem solver—now you have the problem, and they don't.

This brings me to another important negotiating rule: "Never answer an unasked question."

NEGOTIATING RULE

Never answer an unasked question.

The hot potato move is meant to get you to respond to such an unasked question. It is effective only if you start to talk too much and try to provide answers. You've got to be able to toss the potato back where it belongs. Give it back to the person who threw it at you!

Step 1: ARA (Acknowledge, Reassure, and Ask). "That's interesting, and I appreciate you sharing that with me. I'm sorry to hear that. So how are you going to find the other 20%?"

Now you stop talking and wait for them to say something interesting. (Spoiler alert: You will hear something along the lines of "I need your help.")

Step 2: Struggle and Redirect. "Unfortunately," you might say, "I'm struggling here, too. I don't have the 20% you're looking for. I'm thinking this might not work out, and I would understand if that was where you decided to leave this. But before we go there, let me ask you something. When I've been in similar situations in the past, people were able to either recapture the 20% from another project or work with another department to find the funds. What would happen if, on my side, I found a way to lock in this price for the next seven days, and on your side, you did some digging to find a way to recapture the 20% we're looking for?" At this point the prospect will probably return to the idea of you lowering your price right now. You can then move to Step 3.

Step 3: Concessions (Give Something to Get Something). "I understand what you're getting at, and I'm sorry I don't have any more room to move here than you do. It looks to me like we have two options: we decide we're not going to be able to resolve these issues and we can't change the proposal, in which case we're done here; or we re-adjust the solution and remove some of the deliverables. Which of those seems like the best approach here?"

In short, when someone throws you a problem, do you:

A. Try to solve it?

or

B. Ask questions to help them solve it themselves?

You probably answered that you do both, depending on the individual and the circumstances. I do both as well. However, in a negotiation situation your mindset has to be on reversing the discussion back to them so you don't become their rescuer.

Remember: Your job is to stay out of the Drama Triangle.

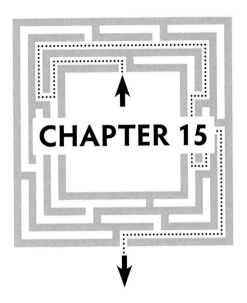

The Emotional Outburst

When you encounter the emotional outburst gambit, the strategic negotiator attempts to manipulate you by sending a message—in person, voice-to-voice, or digitally—that seems totally out of scale and over the top. You are likely to hear (or read an email or text message) something like the following:

- ◆ "Your prices are outrageous!"
- ◆ "I just don't like your solution! It's garbage!"
- ◆ "Your company's service is lousy!"

Again, I would suggest that you go back to what I shared with you back in Chapter 3 about the Drama Triangle. That model, which I suggest that you remind yourself of frequently, will help you keep in mind that these outbursts are tactical maneuvers designed to get you to play the rescuer.

The strategic negotiator is hoping you will automatically apologize for the (possibly nonexistent) problem, hoping to get you to offer up a solution or concession. This trick works so often, so easily, and so well with amateur negotiators that the emotional outburst is one of the most popular moves in the strategic negotiator's arsenal. To overcome it, you must understand why it works so well,

Whenever there is an emotional outburst in a negotiating situation, it is highly likely that the strategic negotiator wants you to choose one of two familiar, less-than-ideal ego states as the starting point of your response. If you respond as a Critical Parent, then you'll be in an argument. Now two people are attempting to overpower each other, but only one of them will be thinking rationally—the strategic negotiator—so that's who will win. If you respond from a need for approval from your Child ego state, you could very well find yourself giving in on a concession too easily. You feel bad about having done something to cause this outburst, and you want to fix it. Again, the strategic negotiator wins, because you aren't thinking rationally.

Neither of those ego states represents a sound strategic choice. Your goal is to remain in your Adult ego state. This, you will recall, is the state that takes the non-emotional road, uses only rational responses, and appeals to verifiable facts to resolve the situation and defuse the emotions.

Before you can practice the tactical side, you have to mentally prepare for this situation by either role-playing or visualizing an emotional situation and becoming clearer and more confident within yourself about how you will respond. I should tell you here and now that, since the emotional outburst gambit is essentially illogical, there is no way to prepare for the specific problem that the strategic negotiator will be freaking out about. Many of these "problems" will be totally nonexistent. The key is to develop some inner certainty on the critical issue of how you will handle inappropriate emotional outbursts, whatever the (supposed) topic is.

I can still recall the period right after I became a sales trainer in 2005. At that time I was 35 and barely looked 30. One of my biggest fears at the time was that I would find myself in front of a business owner who was two or three decades older than I was and who would, at some point, say to me, "What makes you think at your age you could come in here and have an impact on my company?"

Because this was one of my biggest fears, I would practice my response over and over again until I knew I could deliver it under pressure if and when I was ever asked. It went like this: "I appreciate you sharing with me that I'm younger than most of your team, but I'm not here to have an impact on your company. I'm here to have an impact on each individual—and they are here to impact your company." I did run into a couple of strategic negotiators who tried some variation of that line on me during negotiation discussions. (Notice that the outburst had nothing to do with the terms or structure of any training deal; that's the way it is with this gambit. It often connects to nothing of substance.) I kept my cool and delivered my response. It worked.

The lesson: Think about the kinds of emotional situations you could find yourself in when you negotiate. Visualize and imagine the situation, including the kinds of things the strategic negotiator might say and how they would say it. Practice taking a deep breath and responding as an Adult—and then role-play your response with a colleague or manager.

Below is one example of how you could use the playbook to respond effectively, from an Adult ego state, to an emotional outburst gambit. There are countless variations, of course, but the brief summary below will get you started.

Step 1: ARA (Acknowledge, Reassure, and Ask). "Obviously, I surprised you. I just want to make sure you know that was not my intent. Can you please share with me what specifically you feel we need to address again?"

Step 2: Struggle and Redirect. "I hear you, but I have to tell you that I am struggling a little bit about where we go from here. As opposed to walking away, I want to suggest that we take a moment to determine if we can figure out how this went wrong." (Your goal here is simply to move the conversation to something specific—and factual.)

Step 3: Concessions (Give Something to Get Something). "From where I sit, it seems like we have two options: we can decide that we are unable to resolve these issues, in which case you and I are done here, or we re-adjust the proposal and change some of the deliverables to make this something we can work on together. Which of those seems like the best approach here?"

Never forget: The emotional outburst gambit has nothing to do with you, your identity, or your value as a person. It has everything to do with strategy. Bottom line: Your strategy has to be as good as the strategic negotiator's.

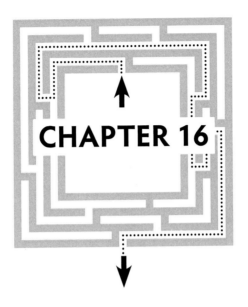

CHAPTER 16

Stonewalling

When you get stonewalled by a strategic negotiator, you find yourself having to deal with a period of unexplained silence following what seemed like a productive meeting, discussion, or exchange. Suddenly there's simply no communication. The phenomenon is also known as being "ghosted." It can happen during a one-on-one conversation; more commonly it happens when a previously predictable stream of text, email, or other communications simply runs dry without any explanation.

The stonewalling technique is typically intended to get you to believe that the opportunity is slipping away—and motivate you to offer concessions without getting anything in return. It is also a favorite late-stage maneuver from professional buyers who have been taught that they've not received the best deal unless you've expressed the willingness to walk away.

When communication ceases, it may well make you feel strongly that the time has come to entice the prospect back to the table with a better offer. I can't tell you how many salespeople I work with who respond to this gambit by texting or emailing the strategic negotiator with a "special" month-end or year-end discount to try to get them to re-engage. Before the freeze-out, no such discount existed. Then the strategic negotiator stopped talking, the salesperson felt rejected, and suddenly the discount materialized. Not a good pattern. This is how margins disappear!

The first and probably most important advice I can share with you on this gambit is to closely consider the following wise observation: "You can't fail at prospecting unless you fail to prospect."* What it means is simple: prospecting is the lifeblood of your income, and there's simply no excuse for ignoring it. Keeping a full pipeline

---

* Source: David Sandler.

will ensure you aren't so desperate for the deal that you are vulnerable to this tactic. If you need a deal, then your problem isn't that they are stonewalling, your problem is that you're failing to prospect at the appropriate level. The idea is to ensure that no one deal is going to make or break you. Once you understand that point, you can proceed to the question of how to deal with this gambit when it surfaces in your world—which it will.

Assuming you have a full pipeline, there are a couple of good options at your disposal when you get stonewalled. What I'm about to share with you is by far the most common situation sellers face today: The strategic negotiator stops returning your texts, voicemails, and emails. You want to figure out what's really happening without falling into the trap of negotiating against yourself, which is what the strategic negotiator wants you to do. If the silence is a tactic, you want to make it clear to the strategic negotiator, in a tactful, mature, and professional manner, that it's not going to work. (That's Goal 1.) If the silence is a signal that the deal has in fact stalled for some reason, you want to find out what that reason is and, if the situation dictates it, close the file. (That's Goal 2.) Let's face it, the outcome that something unexpected happened in the buyer's world and there is simply no deal here is a possibility; your job is to find out whether that's the case.

The best way to pursue each of these goals is to send

text or email messages that complete Step 1 and Step 2 of the playbook in a digital mode, to address Goal 1 and Goal 2, respectively. (You can't execute on Step 3 until there is actual communication in the relationship.) Here's what the message sequence might look like.

Step 1: ARA (Acknowledge, Reassure, and Ask). Send an "It must have been my fault" email. It might read like this: "Hiroki, since we've not been able to reconnect, I want to acknowledge that this may have been because I unknowingly did something that offended you or your company. If that was the case, please know that it was unintentional. Could I ask a favor? Would you let me know if I am right about this, so I can appropriately apologize? After that, we can continue to determine if our company can help yours, and I'll gladly step out of the process and turn the communication over to another colleague." Although this message may seem extreme, it's highly effective. The real message it is sending to the strategic negotiator is, "I'm happy to apologize for something if that will move this discussion forward—but I won't offer unilateral concessions."

Step 2: Struggle and Redirect. Send a "Close the file" email, something like, "Hiroki, we've not been able to reconnect, and I am struggling to figure out why. It may be because you've been busy with other projects. But if this initiative is still a priority for you, I trust I'll hear from you within the next 24 hours. On the other hand, this may no longer be a priority for you personally, and if that's the case it's probably best that I begin to reach out to someone else within your company. If I don't hear from you, I'll presume it's the latter situation. I enjoyed our communication and I'm hopeful our paths will cross again soon."

Even the most accomplished strategic negotiator will likely reach out to you after receiving this message, if only to keep you from taking the discussion elsewhere in the organization. If you hear nothing back after this, the odds are good that you are not looking at a tactic, and that something really has come up internally in the buyer's world that is keeping this discussion from moving forward. It may make sense to connect with other people in the buying organization to figure out what the right next step is.

The key point to remember here is to not give in to the pressure of the silent treatment and start negotiating against yourself. Work the three-step playbook. Figure out what's really going on, and chart an appropriate course once you know.

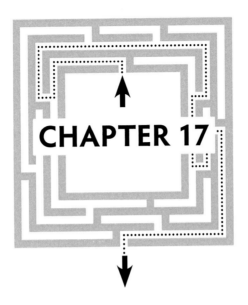

CHAPTER 17

Changing the Cast of Characters

I n this classic gambit of changing the cast of characters mid-negotiation, you work your way forward on any number of substantive issues in the discussion (or seem to), and then you get a message like this: "Sorry. Things have suddenly gotten very busy on my side. I'm going to be handing this project over to my replacement, Person You've Never Met and Don't Know, so you can work out the final details with them."

In comes a new person with a whole new perspective,

someone who hasn't been emotionally or logistically involved in the conversation, someone who doesn't know (or perhaps pretends not to know) what has happened up to this point. Since you have no rapport or trust built with this person, is it any surprise that they quickly start changing the rules—and then start doing their best to make you give concessions you didn't think you would have to make?

Typically, this gambit is executed when there is a procurement department at the company. Your primary point of contact throws the entire engagement over to someone in Procurement, who has zero emotional involvement in the discussions and zero personal history with you. Did you see that coming? No. Could you have? That's what we are here to talk about.

This gambit leaves you feeling like you have very little leverage. You know why that is? Because you don't have leverage. That was the whole idea all along: To reduce your influence on the process. And guess what? If this happens to you, there's no point blaming the strategic negotiator for your situation—because you put yourself in this situation!

That may seem harsh, but consider. You had the chance to set up the ground rules earlier on—and you didn't. That's the only way changing the cast of characters can happen to you: if you fail to set up clear ground rules by executing a good Decision Step as part of your sales process.

You could have found out about the procurement department's role. You could have asked for an introduction. You could have gotten a clear sense of what the decision process looked like for this deal, and you could have made a point of identifying everyone who would be participating in that process, directly or indirectly. You could have built some bridges.

You could also have gotten explicit agreements from the other side about exactly how the discussion would be moving forward and what had to happen on each side in order for that forward movement to occur. You could also have gotten agreements about what either side could do in the event that one side simply started playing by different rules—rules that came out of nowhere, rules that no one ever agreed to up front.

But, you didn't do any of that. That was, let's face it, a strategic error. The strategic negotiator took advantage of that error and pulled this gambit on you. That's reality.

In any negotiation situation, there is always a hidden influencer. Your job is to identify as many of those influencers as you possibly can—before you make a presentation. Think of the last time you made a major purchase like a car, or a house, or even a major appliance. Have you got such a purchase in mind right now? Good. Now answer this next question honestly: How many people did you talk to about that purchase before you made a commitment to buy?

NEGOTIATING RULE

Slow the process down in order
to speed the sale up.

When I ask this question during training programs, the answers that come back tend to range between five and seven, with some people reporting over ten discussions with hidden influencers. Moral: On important decisions, human beings tend to involve other human beings. Is there really any reason to expect that the dynamic will be any different in your world? The more important the decision, the higher the number of people likely to be involved in it. Conduct your due diligence up front. Find out who the influencers are and reach out to each of them. Don't be taken by surprise.

I realize that that's all fine in theory. But what if you do find yourself taken by surprise, and you do need to make some kind of constructive response to this gambit? Fair question. Your only move in that situation is to follow one of the most important negotiating rules: slow the process down in order to speed the sale up.

With that goal in mind, you will only use Step 1 of the playbook here. You will use it with the goal of stopping all negotiations, so you can begin at the very beginning with the new person, in the best possible position. Again: Your aim here is not to negotiate. Your aim here is to push the reset button and go back to the beginning of the whole sales process. You might say something like this:

Step 1: ARA (Acknowledge, Reassure, and Ask). "Great. Thank you for keeping me in the loop. I know what it is like to have a lot of things going on at once! I look forward to meeting with [name]. Naturally, this will delay your timeline with implementing this project, because we're going to have to start back at the beginning so [name] is aware of the impact this project has on your company. Is it possible for the three of us to have a brief hand-off call so that we can all be clear about the agenda items for my initial discussion with [name]?"

Asking this question does a few important things. First and foremost, it makes it clear to the strategic negotiator that the change of rules comes at a price; there will be a delay of as-yet-unknown length because of the decision to make you deal with an entirely new person. Second, it tells the strategic negotiator that you are not going to simply jump through every new hoop the new person presents.

Instead, you are going to follow your own process. Third, it attempts to re-engage the strategic negotiator to take part in the initial discussion with the new person. You may or may not get that engagement, but at this stage it can't hurt to try.

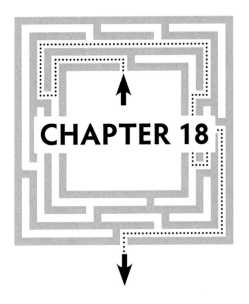

Nibbling

Nibbling, aka incremental negotiating, is when the strategic negotiator makes one or more seemingly minor requests early in the buying discussion—without offering you anything in return. The requests may then escalate. For instance: "Will you be able to throw a few extra licenses in for me?" Or: "Can I get these upgrades at last year's price?"

When someone starts to talk about issues like this, you may feel a sense of relief; they are leaning into the conversation, not away from it, and they want to do business with you. Hooray! The impulse is to be so grateful that you don't know how to thank them.

Guess what? The strategic negotiator has some ideas about how you can thank them: by granting them a couple of tiny concessions right off the bat, and then a couple more, and then a couple more after that. But if you keep giving concessions, you'll keep getting asked for them. The strategic negotiator will nibble away at your position for as long as you let them.

The big question is, why do so many people let them?

Here's the likely answer: Many salespeople are desperate for approval. They want to have proof they can show to their manager that the deal is moving forward, so they fall victim to this gambit, and perhaps even congratulate themselves on how well things are going as they do so. The prospect asked politely for something—and of course the salesperson wants to be polite in return and give them what they ask for.

Negotiation is not about being polite. It is about being an Adult. It is about making the best possible grown-up response, and it is about following an extremely powerful negotiating rule: "When you want to know the future, bring it back to the present."

Here's what that negotiating rule looks like in action.

Step 1: ARA (Acknowledge, Reassure, and Ask). Say something along these lines: "I appreciate you asking if we

> # NEGOTIATING RULE
>
> When you want to know the future,
> bring it back to the present.

can throw that in. So, when it comes time to sit down and go through the proposal, would you like us to spend a few minutes discussing your request?"

That's all you need. Don't bother with Steps 2 and 3 for this gambit. Just keep bringing it back to the present.

Bear in mind that every early concession you grant costs you value on your side; the longer you hold onto anything that is asked for, the more valuable it becomes and the greater leverage you create.

Your ability to push these asks off to the end will cause whatever concessions they are looking for to increase in value, and thus give you additional leverage. I've worked with a lot of people who give concessions early in the process as a way to make the buyer feel like they are getting something early. This always backfires with a strategic negotiator. It signals that you will give concessions in order to keep the discussion going. Bad trade!

By the way, if this gambit comes up before you get to any pricing conversation, that's a flashing red light indicating that you haven't properly completed the Budget Step, which is an important part of the sales process.

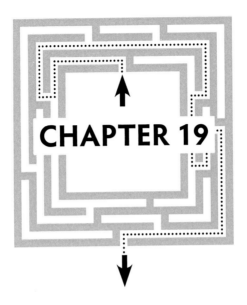

Promise of Escalation

The promise of escalation gambit is a classic margin-killer, one that you are likely to run into when dealing with a prospect with whom you have not done business before. Very early in the discussion, the strategic negotiator will say something like the following: "We have a lot of business we're going to be sending your way, so give us a great deal on this first one."

Make no mistake. The strategic negotiator is messing with your head here, trying to make you feel compelled to do a skinny deal. The assumption here is that you will agree to a huge concession very early on in the relation-ship, simply because you want to get your foot in the door. The question is: Will you?

Beware! This is the dreaded promise of escalation gambit. No matter what the strategic negotiator says will happen later, you can never go back to a higher pricing or return to your original margin model once they know you have the ability to do a deal at a lower rate. You will always be locked into the rate you agree to here. So don't agree to a rate that doesn't support your business plan.

At Sandler, we have a saying: "Never look in your prospect's pocket!" Translation: Don't talk yourself into the proposition that they can't or won't pay you what your solution is worth. They may have a lot of money to work with right now, or they may have a little money. You haven't figured that out yet. The point is to identify what this solution looks like, and see whether it makes sense for both sides. Don't get distracted by the question of whether there is any future business at stake. That's not relevant. Bring yourself back to the present and work the deal at hand.

Do only Steps 1 and 2 of the playbook in this situa-tion. The point here is that you have not yet reached the horse-trading stage, so you are in no position to offer a concession.

Step 1: ARA (Acknowledge, Reassure, and Ask). Say, "Thank you so much for sharing that with me. I have to say, we are really excited about doing business with your company, and I do know there is a lot riding on this. Can I ask you a favor, though, as you and I work to pull together the entire solution? If there is any element of the package that I suggest that you feel is not right, can you commit to sharing that with me, too?" It's very likely that, in response, the strategic negotiator will find a way to reiterate the idea of you offering a concession up front in exchange for some elusive, vague, future deal.

Step 2: Struggle and Redirect. "I want you to know that I do appreciate the opportunity to work with you on an ongoing basis and earn our way to becoming one of your most trusted partners. However, I am struggling a little bit, because I really wouldn't want to compromise any aspect of the solution we put together for you, and frankly, I don't want to start this relationship out on the wrong foot. Let's focus on this opportunity. When we prove to you that we can deliver, then we'll both feel good about working through the next project."

Hold your ground! Do not offer a concession in exchange for the privilege of doing business with the strategic negotiator.

In the next part of the book, I'll show you how to supercharge your Playbook.

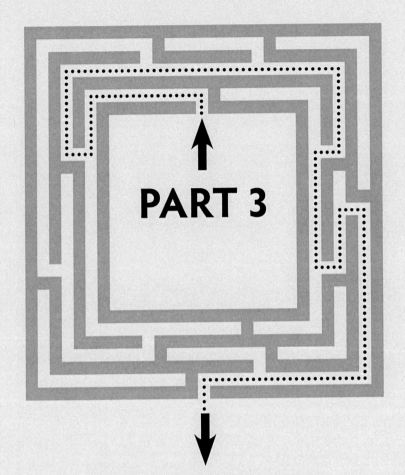

PART 3

Supercharge Your Playbook

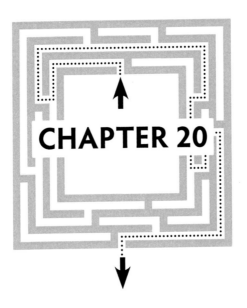

Sources of Leverage

Have you ever entered a negotiation and felt like you just didn't have a leg to stand on? Have you ever found yourself silently praying that your negotiating partner would not ask you for something, because you knew they were in such a position of control in the relationship that you would have to do your best to make anything they asked for happen, whether you wanted to or not?

What about the other side of the table? Have you ever been there? Have you ever felt like you were in such a strong position that if your counterpart asked for something, you knew you didn't have to give it to them? Have you ever been in a position where you knew, deep down, that the other person needed an agreement more than you did?

Either way, what you've experienced was that remarkable negotiating force known as "leverage." Leverage in negotiating is like the undertow when people are out swimming near the beach. You can't see it on the surface, but even so, it's pulling powerfully beneath the surface.

You gain or lose leverage in various ways. If you're not aware of areas where you can gain leverage in the negotiation, then you may be missing opportunities. The goal is to consistently gain leverage and neutralize any weaknesses so that you can be in the strongest position possible. The negotiating discussion is like running a business; as the interactions move forward, you want to build up your leverage assets and limit your leverage liabilities.

Can leverage be quantified? Many people will tell you it can't. However, I believe there are specific kinds of leverage, each of which can be identified, targeted, tracked, and accelerated. Let me explain why I believe that.

I was recently contacted by a group of people who work for a local technology startup accelerator and co-working organization called the Tampa Bay Wave. The Wave is a great organization that provides resources like mentoring, business planning, and investor pitch guidance to startup companies looking to either grow organically or seek funding from angel investors, private equity firms, or both. The reason these people reached out to me was that they wanted me to help these startup companies get better at handling meetings with potential investors.

That's a pretty important priority! Think about it. You are the founder of a startup technology company, and you are trying to seek significant funding from a high net-worth individual, a group of high net-worth individuals, or a private equity company. You're preparing for one of the most important conversations of your life. The people you will be talking to will be making a decision that has a huge impact on you and your world: whether to invest their money in your company or someone else's.

What kind of leverage could you possibly have in that situation? You need the funding to grow and scale your business. The investors have that money. Surely they have all the leverage.

Maybe not. There are ways for you to create leverage in this situation. Following are the seven areas that can serve as sources of powerful leverage in a negotiating discussion. I call them leverage points. Each leverage point can be exploited during negotiation discussions as an asset; conversely, each can be a liability. What I want you to notice is that, in the startup situation, not all of the leverage points are on the side of the prospective investors. Some could be exploited by the founder of the startup.

The idea here is twofold: to identify the liabilities ahead of time so you can resolve them, or at least plan to minimize them during negotiations; and also to identify the assets ahead of time, so you can use them to your advantage during negotiations. Let's take a look at the eight possible sources of leverage that are present in every negotiating situation.

Time

Although there is no formal priority when it comes to acquiring and making good use of leverage, my personal choice for the first one to consider is always time. Time encompasses both the question of when something happens in your world and the question of how the when of what's happening in your world can be coordinated with things that are happening in your negotiating partner's world. I refer to the latter leverage factor as "timing."

Time controls everything in business. The more you understand how time and timing affect you and your negotiating partner, the better you'll be able to strategize the frequency of your discussions and thereby enhance their impact. I've seen managers and salespeople fall into the trap of making time a liability, because they put pressure on themselves to get the deal done by the end of the month/quarter. As the end of the allotted period of time gets closer, they start to make discount offers—and, all too often, come across as desperate.

When would you say the very best time to buy a car is? You guessed it. The end of the month, end of the quarter, or end of the year. That's when the sales team is likely to be under pressure to discount. If you know this and act on it as a buyer, you are using that information as leverage. By the same token, if you let your prospects know that you'd like to have this deal done by the end of the month, you are then weakening your position and conditioning your clients to use this timing against you in future negotiating situations.

In order to strengthen your position with regard to time, downplay any concerns about when the deal is done no matter what pressures you may be under personally. In addition to that, start asking better questions about the buyer's timeframes. For example:

- "When would you like to have this [system, project, etc.] completed?"
- "Why by then?"
- "What happens if it's not done by then?"

It never ceases to amaze me how many salespeople fail to ask these kinds of questions early on in the process and thereby miss an important opportunity to create leverage.

The more you find out about when they'd like to have the project started and their reasons why, the more you make timing an issue for them, and the more likely you are to make time an asset rather than a liability on your side.

Belief

Here's a question for you: Would you buy your own product or service at the rate you're charging?

Here's another one: Do you believe your own time, attention, and expertise is worth the amount you're asking for it?

If you wouldn't or don't, then your belief system is going to get in the way of your ability to stand firm when that is required in a negotiation situation. Your belief system is either an asset or a liability. If it's a liability, you may want to take a close look at reality on the ground and between your ears until your belief system has been upgraded to where it needs to be.

A company I had been working with for about a year had an interesting turnaround when management made the decision to hire an experienced salesperson to join their current team of about 15 sales technicians who did in-home repairs. I'll call this new hire Madelon. Within one month, Madelon was delivering almost 50% more in revenues than the most seasoned veterans on staff. The difference was so stark that some people began to question whether her numbers were real. A brief check of her customer list and paid invoices confirmed that this was no scam. Not only that—her online reviews were consistently higher than the other technicians. This was really happening. Madelon was in fact closing significantly more business than anybody else. The question was: Why?

Was it the territory she was serving? Nope. Was the competition somehow less active within her customer base? Nope. What made the big difference was Madelon's belief system, which was rooted in the following simple principle: "I charge more because I'm worth more—and I'm going to fix your problem right the first time." That core belief was what was enabling her to hit numbers that were never before seen. Slowly, over a period of about six months, others on staff learned, with training and reinforcement, how to shift their beliefs as well, so that they were more in line with Madelon's. Those who did found that they were soon equaling her numbers.

Where is your company positioned in the marketplace? What are your beliefs and attitudes about your company's ability to implement and deliver what you've sold? Naturally, if you don't feel you or your company can deliver, then your leverage during negotiations will suffer.

This is one of those areas of leverage where an entrepreneur such as a startup founder definitely can have a negotiating advantage over a potential investor. In order to secure that advantage, however, you must be willing to identify and uproot any and every disempowering belief you have about yourself, your company, and the market in which you operate—and then take massive, sustained action that is in full alignment with a constructive belief system.

There is a powerful observation I share with my clients (and with everyone else out to make financial success a reality in their lives). Here it is: "You are, at this moment, earning exactly what you believe you're worth, not a penny more or a penny less."* That's an idea to ponder—one that points toward a potentially game-changing area of leverage for you to exploit.

Need

Need is a powerful factor in negotiation that is closely linked to the pain you are able to uncover—the emotional distance between where the buyer is now and where they want to be.

Let me share an example that will illustrate what need looks like in the real world. I grew up in Pennsylvania, but I have lived in Florida for all my adult life. Back when I was a kid living in Pennsylvania when the furnace went out and we didn't have any heat during the winter, our

---

*   Source: David Sandler.

need to get it fixed was great—and therefore my father's ability to negotiate on rates was limited.

Similarly, in Florida, when our air conditioning goes out in July, our need to get it fixed is immediate. That reduces our leverage somewhat when it comes to pushing back on the rates.

Consider those two simple illustrations, then step back for a moment and consider this simple question: How badly does your prospect or counterpart need what you have to offer?

Another way of looking at this is to ask, what is their BATNA? BATNA stands for Best Alternative To a Negotiated Agreement. (The BATNA concept was developed by Roger Fisher and William Ury of the Harvard Program on Negotiation.) If the person you're negotiating with decides not to work with you, what is their next best alternative? Do you know?

In competitive situations, understanding this leverage point usually means looking critically at the strengths, merits, and position of your competition and then strategizing how to better position yourself against them and set yourself apart from them. Corporate buyers, in particular, are eager to make competitive negotiating situations more commodity-focused. If your offering is no different than your competition's, then they'll choose the one with the lowest price. If you offer something that is extremely important to the buyer that can't be obtained anywhere else, need is an asset for you.

On the other hand, let's pretend you need the deal more than they do. Let's pretend that in order to hit your numbers, keep your job, stay in business, whatever, you must close this sale—and your negotiating partner knows that you must. Congratulations: You've created a liability. Naturally, a strategic negotiator will take advantage of this and push you to make major concessions. You can limit this potential vulnerability in a number of ways, such as keeping a full pipeline of opportunities, keeping your financial house in order, and following a plan or playbook that keeps you focused.

Emotion

Have you ever made a purchase decision and then, within 24 hours, found that you were experiencing the classic syndrome of buyer's remorse? I know I have.

As you ponder that question, and perhaps relive a recent example of this phenomenon, take a moment to consider one of the most important negotiating rules: "People buy emotionally and then justify their decisions logically."*

This pattern is in evidence in any and every case of buyer's remorse. People are drawn in emotionally, and

---

*   Source: David Sandler.

then once the emotions recede a bit, the intellectual side of their brain kicks in and they decide they've made an unwise decision.

NEGOTIATING RULE

People buy emotionally and then justify their decisions logically.

Your ability to control your emotions during any negotiation is a potentially huge area of leverage. Knowing when and how to step away from impulsive, emotional responses—especially when that's the kind of reaction the strategic negotiator is hoping to elicit—will help you think straight, put things in the proper perspective, and respond with the right tactics and strategies.

You are more likely to make a mistake when you are driven by emotions. But learning to step away from emotion is something that each and every strategic negotiator has mastered. You can master it, too.

One great way not to get too emotionally involved in a negotiation is to have a partner or team involved. Outside influences can help you see things from a different perspective and help you minimize or eliminate the negative impact of emotional responses when the stakes are high. Someone in the negotiation is going to have an advantage when it comes to controlling personal emotions. Why shouldn't it be you?

Make a point of studying the emotions of your counterpart. How are they reacting during your initial engagements and conversations? What kind of feelings are you observing? Are they excited, desperate, frustrated, worried, concerned? Are they using emotionally charged words throughout your conversation? (For instance, do they express authentic anger or use the word "angry" about some situation they are facing?) Notice these nuances. Keep your head, and you can put yourself in a better leveraged position later on in the negotiation process.

Relationship

Would you be likely to negotiate harder or easier with someone you knew really, really well?

Naturally, some people will make choices that prove to be the exception, but the reliable rule that I have seen play out is that the more I know and trust someone, and the more they know and trust me, the less likely they are to expect major concessions from me. They are far more likely to feel they are already receiving a fair deal from a person they know and trust. They want to support and sustain the relationship with me over time. This factor of the strength and quality of the relationship also determines the leverage present in the relationship. Sellers experience it largely in the (common) phenomenon of a first-time buyer presenting a tough set of conditions that must be met in order to get signoff on the first project. If they aren't going to push around a brand new contact, who are they going to push around?

David H. Maister, the author of *The Trusted Advisor*, offers this formula for those eager to build trust in a relationship:

$$T = \frac{C \times R \times I}{SO}$$

Let's define the terms in this equation. **T = Trust.** What about the rest of it?

C = Credibility. Obviously, you wouldn't be inclined to trust someone you can't believe. The same goes for your potential negotiating partner. What can you do to build credibility throughout your interaction with them? Good answers to this question include: sharing stories from, and access to, happy customers; sharing articles, reviews, and awards that spotlight your company's performance and strong suits; and telling the truth, no matter what.

R = Reliability. No surprise here. Doing what you say you are going to do raises the level of trust in the relationship. This is one area where your personal style, history, and example can have a huge impact on the other person's perception of your entire organization. If you say you're going to show up on time for the meeting or conference call and you make a point of doing that, the other person's perception of your organization's reliability is likely to improve. The better the long-term experience of being able to count on you in matters big and small, the higher your perceived reliability. The quicker and more effective your service response when there's a problem, the higher your perceived reliability.

I = Intimacy. This aspect of the trust equation is all about how well the other person knows you as an individual, and vice versa. Inevitably, the intimacy factor touches on the world beyond your work identity. Have you shared some aspect of that part of yourself—appropriately? Of course, this is always a balancing act, because too much information about your family or personal life is going to be a problem in a business context, as is too little. But you should share something. By the same token, have you gotten to know your counterpart socially, or at the very least checked out their Facebook and LinkedIn pages, to have some small-talk material? Another great way to build intimacy is to cast aside any presumptions of your own infallibility that you may have inadvertently indulged in and open up just a bit about your shortcomings or mistakes. Being a little vulnerable in a business setting may not come easily to you at first, but it is a great way to improve intimacy.

SO = Self-Orientation. Keeping this low is the foundation principle. As a matter of habit, do you keep the focus on yourself and what you know, or do you make a point of shining the spotlight of attention on the other person? Remember the 70-30 rule: 70% of the time the other person should be talking and 30% of the time you should be talking. Basic stuff, I know, but in my experience, way too many people like to talk about themselves in negotiation settings.

Put it all together, and it equals trust. As you build trust over time, their impulse to negotiate harder with you will diminish simply because of the improved quality of the relationship.

Understanding

You might not have thought of understanding as a source of leverage, but it is a powerful one.

Are you able to put yourself in your counterpart's world and understand their point of view, their business, their industry, their market, their motives? When they take a certain negotiating position, do you understand what made them take that position? Do you understand the kinds of chess moves that their leadership is trying to make? Do you understand their mission?

Yes, all of this is easier said than done. Gaining leverage in this area requires you to do some research and spend some time being an investigator. But you will find, I believe, that it is an investment that pays off huge dividends.

What you are looking to understand first is the big picture. What is the organization's mission? What is the ultimate goal they are trying to achieve? Understanding what their business is trying to achieve by purchasing your products and services is essential. It all comes down to effective questioning. Questions that help you and the other person to "monetize" the problem as it stands—that is, figure out how much leaving it unsolved actually costs—are particularly important here. Asking such questions sometimes intimidates salespeople, since the monetization process begins with fundamental questions like, "Is doing nothing an option?" But if you don't get an honest answer to a question like that, you won't be able to get an honest answer to later questions that identify just how much direct and indirect financial benefit is connected to adopting your solution. You also won't gain a real-world understanding of why it does (or doesn't) make sense to work together.

The better understanding you have of their situation, the more prepared you will be when they take a certain negotiating position. For example, when someone attempts to negotiate your price down, they are taking a position. But notice: Their mission is not to get a lower price. Their mission is to do X, whatever X is, and to find a solution to the challenge that is keeping them from doing that at peak efficiency. The more closely attuned you are to their mission and to how your solution can help them fulfill it, the better your responses will be to any subsequent positions—and the more leverage you will gain.

Ownership

Ownership in this context means personal, emotional investment in the solution that is being proposed or discussed.

You gain leverage in any negotiation situation whenever the other side puts their fingerprints on the solution being developed—by their making a suggestion or revision, by asking others in their organization to provide feedback, or by adding an idea of their own to one of your ideas. Effective negotiators are good at soliciting fingerprints.

Before you make a formal recommendation, stop and ask yourself: Is any part of what you are about to propose co-created by you and the prospect in order to involve ownership on both sides? If the answer is no, you are giving up leverage.

Your goal is to create deeper and deeper ownership of your solution throughout the interaction cycle by involving all parties in discussions and building their input into the solution. You want them to feel that they own the solution. If you are the only one who feels full emotional ownership—for instance, because you have placed all your chips on this one deal and have positioned yourself in a "must win" situation—then you lose leverage. By the same token, you've lost leverage when you've become so enamored with your company, product, or service that you refuse to change anything and make no effort to involve your counterpart's ideas in the process.

Let your counterpart define their own solution, so you can see what their version of the solution would look like. Getting them involved in shaping the solution, getting them to assume greater and greater ownership of the eventual outcome, shifts the leverage in your favor and creates deeper buy-in to the idea of working with you.

For example, when I have a prospect in my pipeline whose situation requires that our training delivery involve a number of geographic locations and different team members—for instance, business development representatives, account managers, account executives, and sales leaders—one of the first questions I ask is, "What are your thoughts about how we're going to deliver training to these teams consistently?" This question starts a conversation that allows them to share with me, at length, their vision of how the training can be effective for these varied teams. I take plenty of notes. I let the other person share everything that seems relevant. Then, and only then, do I share my own best practices of working with a remote team of professionals. That's how the co-creating begins.

Skill

Your own level of skill, familiarity, and comfort in the realm of negotiation is a huge potential area of leverage. When you are negotiating with a strategic negotiator, your best-case scenario is going to be establishing equal leverage in this area. Consider that a victory of sorts—at least you're not playing at a disadvantage.

Negotiation is a skill. It takes time and practice and persistence to reach a stage of mastery with it. Like anything else you've ever become good at, you will have to put in the time if you want to maximize your skill level. So ask yourself this: When was the last time you practiced negotiation? There may be many more opportunities to practice than you are now taking advantage of.

I enjoy playing golf. Every time I go to check-in at the pro shop before the round, I'll ask the person behind the counter, "What kind of discounts are available?" I purposely make this an open-ended question, one that helps to lead the person into the mindset of figuring out what discounts they provide on a regular basis. This always leads into a discussion about what is available. Sometimes, there are not any discounts that I qualify for. But, more often than not, we figure out a discount of some kind that can be applied. By doing this, I'm not only practicing the art of the negotiating conversation, I'm also saving some money on golf.

It's amazing how often that simple question starts a good discussion. I realize that you may not play golf, but there are plenty of other ways to practice that you can consider. For instance:

- Ask whether there are any discounts available for regular customers the next time you take your pet to the veterinarian.

- Go to the car dealership and ask for a test drive, even though you aren't in the market for a car. Who knows? They might be experiencing the end-of-the-month blues and might make you an offer you have to think twice about walking away from.

- If you have routine vendors at your company, offer to reach out to them to negotiate the next contract.

Another great way to hone your negotiation skills is by role-playing on a regular basis with colleagues. By running through various negotiation scenarios on a regular basis with your team, you can consistently practice your skills. Many people I work with tell me that they dislike role-playing of any kind. I often hear things like, "I never do it that way when I'm in front of a client," or "It's much more difficult to do it in front of my peers than it is with an actual client." Simply put, these are excuses that come about as the result of not doing enough role-playing. For a couple of our training clients, we've stopped calling it role-playing and call it "practice." If that works for you, great! Find a colleague or a manager and start practicing the concepts and strategies I've shared with you on a regular basis. Put it in your calendar. Once a week for fifteen minutes is a good way to start.

In the next chapter, I'll share some insights on the most common mental errors that undermine attempts at negotiation.

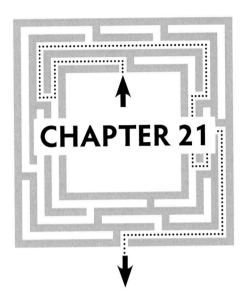

CHAPTER 21

The Seven Errors That Undermine Negotiations

I n this chapter, I challenge you to start noticing the potentially serious mistakes people make during negotiating discussions. It's very likely that one or more of the mistakes we'll be looking at are ones that you've made in the past. If you can understand the most common mistakes that show up in your own negotiation process, then you'll be able to recognize them, own them, and avoid them the next time—and you'll be better positioned to capitalize on them when your adversaries make these same mistakes. Although there are many mistakes to be made, I've identified seven that we at Sandler have determined are most likely to undermine a negotiation discussion.

1. Failure to Recognize a Strategic Negotiator

Most business negotiations happen over a period of interactions through either the buying or selling cycle. During this time, be aware of the personas of the people or team you're are dealing with. Failing to recognize early on that you are dealing with a strategic negotiator (or a team of strategic negotiators) will put you at a strategic disadvantage.

We have already talked about how to recognize the strategic negotiator and the best ways to prepare yourself for negotiations with this person in Chapter 6. I am placing this item at the head of the list of possible mistakes as an important reminder for you to go back and closely review that chapter, as well as all of Part 2 of this book, which outlines the twelve most likely gambits the strategic negotiator is likely to throw your way, before you enter into any negotiation.

2. A Weak Pre-Negotiation Position

There are countless factors that can weaken your position early on in the negotiation process, but by far the most common factor is your own belief system. This issue is covered in depth in the previous chapter, under the heading "Belief." I will only add here that one of the most common mental errors I have seen people make in negotiation settings is the belief that they have less status or worth than the person with whom they are negotiating. This is what we at Sandler call "head trash." Whether you have acknowledged it to yourself yet or not, you really do have a right to be at the negotiating table; you really do have equal business stature with your negotiating partner. The only question is whether you will claim and make good use of that equal business stature. Too many business professionals don't. They are victims of their own head trash. For more on this vitally important topic, let me suggest that you take a few minutes to check out this podcast, which deals with the topic in depth: www.sandler.com/blog/creating-equal-business-stature.

3. Making Unilateral Concessions

A friend of mine was out visiting a furniture store a while back. He wanted to buy a sofa. The salesperson at the store who was answering his questions knew all the features about the sofa my friend was looking at backwards and forwards and was having loads of fun reciting those features. After a couple of minutes of this, my friend nodded, looked the salesperson in the eye, and said, "You know what, this model looks pretty good to me. What do I do now?"

Has there ever been an easier response from which to close a sale? I don't think so.

This makes what happened next all the more amazing. According to my friend, who has no reason to lie about this, the salesperson flinched a little bit, avoided looking him in the eye, and then said, "I can only knock a hundred dollars off the list price."

Sure. Why not?

Funny story. Kind of. (Actually, when you stop to think of it, the level of head trash necessary for someone to give away a hundred bucks' worth of margin when the deal is basically closed is pretty unfortunate.) But be honest: doesn't that story illustrate a point that is relevant to everyone who sells for a living? If you've never even been tempted to give up something without getting something in return, you have my congratulations. But most of the people I work with have some work to do in this area.

Am I saying you should never add value to a prospect's day? Of course not. If, early on during your interaction and before you begin any negotiations, you can give something to your counterpart that builds the relationship and helps you to establish a level of trust, something that is given at little or no cost to you, then go for it. This is a great tactic that can pay off later in the negotiation process. For example, you might provide specific insight to a problem they have in the company, industry, or marketplace, insight you can offer due to your experience with working with companies similar to theirs. Or perhaps you conduct an audit or assessment of their current situation that will be seen by them as valuable—and at the same time enhance their clarity about the need for your solution. That kind of "gift" can prove to increase your leverage. But that's not what I mean by making unilateral concessions.

A good negotiator is going to ask you for concessions early. Your success lies in not giving up early in these discussions—and certainly not volunteering to give a concession!

When pressed for a concession early on, your standard comment needs to sound something like this: "I appreciate you asking for us to include or consider _____. When we get to the point of discussing how all of this is going to come together, then we'll address this."

Hold on to that concession until later in the process. Remember, the longer you hold onto something, the more valuable it becomes in the negotiating process.

Another unfortunate scenario I see quite often with my clients is the back-and-forth dance a sales representative does with their sales manager in order to get a deal done. The prospect is asking for concessions, discounts, special terms, and so on—and the salesperson's best negotiating tactics end up being used on the manager, in order to meet the prospect's demands. This is never a good cycle to fall into. The only time it is appropriate is when you have first gained a clear commitment from your counterpart that if X concession is granted, the deal is done. Even then, the concession should come about as the result of the prospect giving something, too.

4. Talking Too Much

You've probably heard the saying, "The first person who talks loses." I don't believe that is necessarily true in negotiations. If the first person is astute enough to ask the other person a good question, that may lead to a win. But the point here is to get the other person talking. If you are talking at length during the negotiation process, that means the other person is listening and gathering information—not us. So talking too much really is a major problem. I've never heard of anyone listening themselves out of a deal.

Typically, salespeople talk too much because they are trying to defend or justify their position, their product, or their solution. Again: You should only be talking 30% of the time. To avoid talking too much, start planning your questions early. The more time you spend identifying the right questions to ask, questions that will help you to gain the insights and information you would like to have, the more information you will uncover.

Think of yourself as a reporter. You're about ready to interview a major celebrity. How much time would you take to prepare? What kind of research would you do? Quite a lot, right? The same goes here. Don't fall into the trap of focusing all your energy on figuring out what you're going to say—focus on what you are going to ask.

There are two important categories of questions to prepare.

Strategic Questions

These are designed to focus on the big picture. They help uncover the vision and real purpose of what is going to be accomplished. For example:

- "How does this project affect your business overall?"
- "What will a successful outcome do to increase revenues for the business?"
- "When you've done other projects like this before, what were some of the best practices you developed for working with an outside partner?"

Tactical Questions

These are more specific questions about a certain issue

or situation that needs to be drilled down into in order to determine the depth of a specific concern. This kind of question allows you to probe beneath the surface of a particular problem. For example:

- ◆ "Can you tell me more about that issue?"
- ◆ "Could you give me an example of what you mean by X?"
- ◆ "The last time this situation occurred, what did you do?"

There is a lot more to this topic, of course. I could write a whole book on the topic of asking your prospect effective questions, but fortunately, someone else has.*

5. Losing Control of Your Emotions

Consider this scenario. You've spent a lot of time, energy, and effort to seal a deal, and you think you have it won. But at the last minute you are faced with a "take it or leave it" demand, perhaps based on the "our budget was just slashed by 30% but we still need this so can you please lower your price" move you learned about in Chapter 14. Naturally, you've become emotionally involved in the deal. Naturally, you feel frustrated at this point. Even so,

---

*   Check out Antonio Garrido's excellent *Asking Questions the Sandler Way.*

step back and ask yourself a question: Do you want to react—or respond?

If you lose control by reacting quickly and emotionally to your counterpart, you will probably end up either giving in to the demand and giving away margin needlessly, not giving in and alienating your counterpart, or sometimes even both. A fight or flight response is understandable, but even though these are deeply woven into your DNA, neither is your best move here. The best action at this point is to freeze and do nothing until you either calm down and can respond with a well-thought-out plan or you have the time to consult a manager or peer about the best way to respond.

Responding makes strategic sense. Reacting emotionally doesn't. It's too expensive!

6. Being Unprepared

Some important negotiations drag on for months and then reach a moment of truth that happens very fast, with the critical terms being finalized in a matter of minutes. These situations highlight the vital importance of doing the appropriate prep work up front.

In a typical enterprise sale, which is one that is considered a large sale with multiple buyers and sellers involved and usually higher dollars and longer contract periods, you may have a sales cycle of 6–18 months or longer, requiring numerous face-to-face meetings, phone conversations, and emails. Additionally, multiple decision makers come in and out of the cycle with various points of view and negotiating styles.

Throughout this lengthy process, you must be identifying and cataloguing potential concessions on both sides. When the moment comes to negotiate the terms, and it may come very quickly indeed, you want to be prepared. One of the ways to ensure you are prepared is to document the value and the advantages you bring to the relationship well ahead of time and to update the list regularly. Here are a few items that you may want to keep in mind:

- What does this solution solve for the prospect?
- How does your solution impact the prospect?
- Will the customer save money with your solution or will it help them make money, and how much?
- What part of your solution is the most important to the prospect?
- How good is your competition at solving the prospect's problems, and what advantages do you have?
- What is the level of urgency the prospect has? (Is it more than yours?)
- Have you created a list of concessions that will be of value to the prospect?

Being prepared takes time and thought. Invest that time and thought. You may think you know all of the answers to these questions in your head, but it is all too easy to miss something important. Get it all down in black and white, so you can make the right move when you are under the pressure of an unscheduled discussion with the strategic negotiator. (That, by the way, is a classic late-stage gambit.)

7. Thinking That Money Is the Real Issue

During a question-and-answer period at a technology association, the chief information officer of a local city said something fascinating. She said, "In my world, I absolutely need all of my vendors and partners to believe that the lowest price wins because I work for a public government entity. However, I can assure you that I would have lost my job a long time ago if I only based my buying decision on the lowest price. The best solution to my problem always wins, but I still need to get it for the best price." You could have heard a pin drop—she had some vendors in the room! The point I am making here is: Clients may say pricing is all that matters, but the reality is inevitably more complicated.

Your own attitude and programming about money and your resulting comfort level when discussing money play an important role here. A question I often ask my clients is, "What was it like when you were, say, fifteen years old, talking about money with your parents?" When you were being raised, you learned the concept of money from those who were raising you. Most of the answers I hear from people are that the parents or guardians didn't talk openly about money at all. My belief is that this happened because their parents never talked to them openly about money. So the cycle continues. For most people, money is a taboo subject.

Interactions with parents and other authority figures often determine the healthiness or unhealthiness of a person's own money concept in later life. On the healthy concept side, I hear comments from clients like:

- "Save your money, because you never know when you are going to need more than what you have."
- "If you want something, you are going to have to work for it."
- "I had everything I needed but didn't get everything I wanted."
- "If you are going to buy something for yourself, make sure it lasts."

On the not so healthy side, I hear comments like:

- "Money is the root of all evil."
- "We don't have any, so don't ask for any."
- "One of my parents spent it, the other saved it."
- "Money was the primary cause of my parent's divorce."

All of this leads to some interesting questions. Do you openly and comfortably discuss money with your significant other? If you have children, how are you shaping their beliefs about money? Do you have a mindset of scarcity or of abundance as it relates to money? Is it possible that working on your own beliefs about money will help you the next time you're faced with a good negotiator who asks you for a discount—and who knows, maybe in other areas of your life?

What's important to grasp, on both a mental and an emotional level, is that money is never the real issue. Solving the client's problem is the real issue. Operating from this mindset is vitally important, because it will allow you to shift any negotiation about money back to the real problem of solving the problem. This is a mindset shift first and a tactical shift second. An important part of that shift is opting to make product- or service-based concessions (in exchange for a concession from the other side, of course) instead of agreeing to a concession on price. When the other side asks for a price concession, counter with a concession that involves a change in the product or service mix—and get something in return. (See the discussion about the Negotiation Matrix in Appendix A.)

If you believe, deep down in your gut, that money is the real issue, then you're going to give in to the very first request for a lower price simply because you'd rather not talk about money anyway. On the other hand, if you believe, down deep, that what you're really working out with your negotiating counterpart is the solution that makes the most sense to both sides, then anything is possible.

Epilogue

What matters most in any negotiation situation, I believe, is the inner game: what your self-concept is, how you process information, whether you react or respond to stressful situations, and so on. You must look inside, and keep looking inside, if you want to make the most of your potential as a negotiator. Without this deep and ongoing exploration of your own mental attitudes, applying the tactics and techniques that I've shared with you in this book may be difficult. In high-pressure situations, you are likely to revert back to behaviors that don't support you.

How, then, do you take this information and get the most you possibly can from it? How do you reach your full potential?

I believe the only way you're going to be able to apply these techniques under pressure is by practicing. Over the next few months, I would suggest that you look at most everything you buy as negotiable. Use one of the gambits, ask for a concession, and then watch what the other person does. How do they react? What's their first move? You'll quickly be able to recognize if the person is an amateur, a tactical, or a strategic negotiator.

If you have the opportunity to role-play with peers and superiors at your company about real-world negotiating situations, then I would urge you to schedule some time with them to hone your skills. The more you practice what you have learned in this book with your peers, the more comfortable you'll be when faced with a real negotiating situation. Becoming a strategic negotiator is no different than becoming a top athlete, or a top musician, or any other kind of top performer—the more you practice, the better you'll be able to perform when it's time. Of course, if you want to reach out to us at Sandler.com, you will find that we are all about compressing the learning curve.

Whatever you decide to do, keep practicing, keep learning, and keep growing. I hope this book has helped to make learning and growth a reality in your life.

Appendix A

The Negotiation Matrix

The Negotiation Matrix is a simple, powerful tool you can use to prepare for and respond effectively to requests for concessions from the other side. The idea here is to work out, ahead of time and in writing, a private memo to yourself that reminds you of the list of concessions you are willing to give and what the parallel concessions from the other side might look like. Filling in the blanks on the Negotiation Matrix before you engage in any "horse trading" will solidify in your mind the concessions that you are prepared to make in order to move discussions forward. It will also help you establish the comparable dollar values of your concessions so you can discuss them with the other side when the opportunity arises to do so.

Notice that, in the sample Negotiation Matrix filled out below, the option of discounting the base quoted price is not listed as one of the five possible options. This is because your goal is always to change the product and service mix instead of discounting the quoted price. A blank version for you to copy and use is on the next page.

NEGOTIATING MATRIX

FOR NEGOTIATING WITH: _____ ABC, INC. _____

CONCESSIONS WE COULD OFFER   CONCESSIONS WE WANT FROM THEM

Our order of preference	Concession	Cost to us	Our order of preference	Concession	Value to us
1	Provide additional training	$2,500	1	Place 20% larger order	$20,000
2	Upgraded support plan/ extended warranty	$5,000	2	Agree to pay within 30 days	$10,000
3	Longer access to free customer support	$5,000	3	Agree to pay within 60 days	$7,500
4	Lock in current pricing for 6 months on reorders	$7,500	4	Give us a written and video testimonial upon first delivery	$5,000
5	Lock in current pricing for 12 months on reorders	$10,000	5	Give us one written testimonial upon first delivery	$2,500

NEGOTIATING MATRIX

FOR NEGOTIATING WITH: _____

CONCESSIONS WE COULD OFFER   **CONCESSIONS WE WANT FROM THEM**

Our order of preference	Concession	Cost to us	Our order of preference	Concession	Value to us
1			1		
2			2		
3			3		
4			4		
5			5		

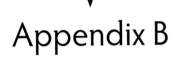

Appendix B

On Negotiating Remotely

I n any negotiating scenario, your ideal is to be conducting the discussions face-to-face in the same room together. That is the optimum environment. Very often, however, you don't have the option of negotiating face-to-face and must create the best alternative environment. To do that, it helps to understand what I call the negotiating environment hierarchy. This is outlined in the table you see below.

QUALITY LEVEL	NEGOTIATING ENVIRONMENT
Ideal	Face-to-face, in same room
Slightly less than ideal	Video conference
Acceptable	Voice-to-voice on telephone (or video conference where cameras are shut off due to technical or bandwidth issues)
Less acceptable	Email
Worst case scenario	Text

The strategy you want to pursue whenever you find yourself dealing with a remote negotiating situation is to get agreement from the other side to move the environment up at least one level from where you are right now. Do this before you discuss the specifics of a proposal or concession.

So for instance, if the other side sends you an email message requesting that you "work on your pricing and send something back to us via email," your first priority is not to address that request directly or to deal with the gambit in any way. Rather, your first priority should be to request, briefly and directly, a video or phone discussion with your counterpart so you can both talk about what happens next. (Notice that a phone conversation is one level above the email level in the table above, and that a video conference is two levels above.)

Work your way up the ladder before you attempt to respond to the gambit. Do your best to secure the best possible environment for the negotiating discussion.

Appendix C

Case Study

Sandler Negotiating Process Leads to Multi-Million-Dollar Enterprise Deal

The below is by Michael Franko, account executive for SentryOne, a leading provider of database performance monitoring and data-ops solutions, who shared the following true story with us.

In our world, a ton of work goes into technically validating an enterprise software offering in the months leading up to final negotiations. In one particular case, we were working with a major prospect, an air carrier, side by side with our tech team. Following Sandler's process, we made sure the budget was discussed up front. If technical agreement was reached, the airline would set aside the funds necessary to secure the purchase.

After a lot of work from both sides, the technical protocols for the software rollout were reached and the funds were allocated. In practice, however, my experience is that the people in procurement often find a way to push back on the price that's been built into the proposal, even though the funds have been allocated. The dialogue in this case went something like the following.

Procurement Officer: Here at [large airline carrier], we seldom do business with less than a 20% discount from what you are offering. Your current proposal falls under this threshold, and we believe we are far from a commercial arrangement.

Us: We wholeheartedly understand what a large airline carrier's stance on software purchases of this magnitude is likely to be. ["Acknowledge, reassure, and ask" is Step 1. Notice that we just acknowledged and reassured their position.] Can I ask you something? [We just asked a question as a softening statement for another question, which is to come.] Up to this point, we have conducted an extensive technical process to prepare all your internal teams for a major shift in how you conduct business. Everything from routes, fares, and equipment availability are going to be tracked through your substantial system investments. Prior to our initial engagement, the leadership was well aware of our initial and year-one costs, and we did gain budget allocation for this initiative. Does that enter into the conversation here? [There was our question.]

Procurement Officer: Well, I don't know about any of that. My feeling is that we are at an impasse as I cannot write the purchase order with the current assigned discounts.

Us: We completely understand your position. At the same time, we are struggling a little bit, because this is a major organizational change that will definitely have an impact if your technical teams are not enabled. But perhaps this isn't the best arrangement for [large airline carrier]; I will go back to our business and technical teams and let them know we will not be moving forward as planned. [Notice that we just struggled and redirected, which is Step 2. The tricky thing about redirecting is, you have to be willing to follow through on it. That's exactly what we had to do when the procurement officer said the following.]

Procurement Officer: Yes, that makes sense. I'm sorry we couldn't reach agreement here.

Us: We certainly appreciate your consideration for our offering.

So we shook hands and walked away from the deal. Or did we?

I called all my stakeholders and let them know where things stood. I shared the dialogue we had had with procurement. Then something interesting happened. Three days before the quarter ended, the airline's business and technical teams weighed in. They explained to Procurement the importance of having this offering in place prior to the end of the quarter. At that point, we heard from Procurement.

Procurement Officer: After careful consideration, it has been deemed necessary to revisit the current agreement that we spoke about earlier this month. We think we can get there if you are able to reduce your current proposal by five percentage points.

Us: We certainly appreciate your willingness to consider our proposal once again. We can raise this concession with our leadership team, but the first thing they are going to ask us is whether this will be completed this month, because in our signed quote and purchase order, we are predicating that the agreement will be in place by the 30th. The second thing they will ask about is whether you would consider a two-year agreement, as most of the heavy lifting of installation and configuration will be an ongoing effort in year one. [This was Step 3, concessions, the give-something-to-get-something step. Of course, we were prepared to ask for both these concessions well ahead of time, because we fully expected to be asked for a concession on price.]

Procurement Officer: I believe we can get this done if the request for a five-point price reduction can be solidified shortly.

Us: Got it. Let me just clarify something, though. This current proposal is only valid if the outlined components are executed by the 30th. Is that fair?

Procurement Officer: Yes, we will do all we can to expedite, and we will look into confirming a two-year agreement.

Us: Thank you. I will be back in touch soon after I am able to present this concession.

This story has a happy ending. The multi-million-dollar contract was executed, the two-year term was agreed upon, and the revenue was recognized in quarter. Note that this transaction would certainly have failed if the technical teams involved had not been engaged and pursuing the same goal as the sales team. That's one of the critical points we learned from Sandler and Clint: to make sure the tech team and the sales team are fully aligned at every step of the sales and negotiation process and to make sure to engage the parallel teams on the other side of the deal.

Look for these other books on shop.sandler.com:

SALES SERIES
The Art and Skill of Sales Psychology
Asking Questions the Sandler Way
Bootstrap Selling the Sandler Way
Call Center Success the Sandler Way
Digital Prospecting
The Contrarian Salesperson
LinkedIn the Sandler Way
Prospect the Sandler Way
Retail Success in an Online World
Sandler Enterprise Selling
The Sandler Rules
The Unapologetic Saleswoman
Why People Buy
You Can't Teach a Kid to Ride a Bike at a Seminar

MANAGEMENT SERIES
Change the Sandler Way
Customer Service the Sandler Way
Lead When You Dance
Motivational Management the Sandler Way
Misery to Mastery
The Intentional Sales Manager
The Right Hire
The Road to Excellence
The Sales Coach's Playbook
The Sandler Rules for Sales Leaders
The Success Cadence
Transforming Leaders the Sandler Way
Winning from Failing

MOTIVATIONAL SERIES
Accountability the Sandler Way
From the Board Room to the Living Room
Sandler Success Principles
Succeed the Sandler Way

INDUSTRY SERIES
Making Channel Sales Work
Patient Care the Sandler Way
Selling in Manufacturing and Logistics
Selling Professional Services the Sandler Way
Selling to Homeowners the Sandler Way
Selling Technology the Sandler Way

NEGOTIATING MASTERY

Negotiating Mastery is a nine-lesson course on how to reach win-win agreements. It is designed for owners, managers, and salespeople who routinely put together complicated deals, negotiate discounts, or engage in enterprise selling.

While this course is based primarily around sales negotiations, it will also be helpful to managers and owners negotiating any type of contract.

The goal of negotiating is to reach an agreement that satisfies both parties and moves the relationship forward, such that each side feels that the other has been fair. In order to achieve this, each side needs to uncover a better understanding of what the other really wants. The best test of a true win/win outcome is whether or not each party would want to enter into additional negotiations with the other in the future. A Sandler-trained salesperson knows how to get a good deal and leave the other side feeling not only that they negotiated a good deal, but that they would be happy to do business again.

This course includes:

- How to negotiate effectively
- Understanding and dealing with the professional negotiator
- Identifying sources of negotiating leverage
- How personality, style, and persuasion affect outcomes
- The most common negotiating mistakes
- The top 12 gambits buyers use and their countermeasures
- Breaking through apparent impasses
- Making concessions
- Preparing for your next negotiation

You will also get access to Sandler's E-Learning Library, an online library of the best of Sandler's sales tips and success principles.

www.sandler.com/negotiating-mastery